SILICONE INJURY

SILICONE INJURY

Memoir of a Life
and of a Spiritual Journey

Hermitra Elan*tra Vedenetra

authorHOUSE®

AuthorHouse™ LLC
1663 Liberty Drive
Bloomington, IN 47403
www.authorhouse.com
Phone: 1-800-839-8640

Published by AuthorHouse   07/19/2013

ISBN: 978-1-4817-5777-5 (sc)
ISBN: 978-1-4817-5778-2 (e)

Library of Congress Control Number: 2013909876

TABLE OF CONTENTS

Preface...vii
Introduction: In the Beginning 1957-1977 ix

PART I - NEW JERSEY.......................................*1*

1 - Living with Implants 1977-1988 3
2 - CFS – Chronic Fatigue Syndrome 1989 11
3 - Stabilization..15
4 - The Truth Is Revealed...................................21
5 - Explant 1992...25
6 - The Correct Diagnosis..................................31
7 - MCS – Multiple Chemical Sensitivity 35
8 - Detoxing and Dancing 1993 41
9 - Spiritual Healing 47
10 - Money Matters 53
11 - Daily Life 1993-1996 59
12 - The Goddess Room......................................65
13 - Descent into Hell 1997-1999 73
14 - Escape 1999 81

PART II - TEXAS...*91*

15 - Success...93
16 - Community...99
17 - The Camp..107

PART III - ARIZONA *115*

18 - Prescott, Arizona 2001................................117
19 - Destiny...123

20 - Purpose...129
21 - Love Story 137
22 - Progression of Silicone Poisoning.....................145
23 - Final Thoughts and Reflections 155

Appendix A: Update on Silicone Breast Implants.....161
Appendix B: References, Books, and Resources........167

PREFACE

This is the story of my life and how it was irrevocably shaped by chemical injury. Chemical injury can happen in many ways. Mine happened through silicone gel breast implants which bled, ruptured and leaked inside my body over the course of fifteen years. The result was catastrophic disease.

This memoir chronicles my medical and physical journey through the symptoms of chronic fatigue syndrome, fibromyalgia, connective tissue/rheumatic disease, multiple chemical sensitivity and electromagnetic hypersensitivity. But most importantly, it recounts the concurrent emotional, psychological and spiritual journeys I undertook to survive my circumstances and make sense of my life.

I decided to write my story after receiving a diagnosis of brain lesions, which significantly hamper my brain processes. This will be evident in my writing. And due to my inability to use computers, I wrote it all the old-fashioned way: long-hand.

This may not be the easiest story to read, but it's important for the world to know the impact and degree of devastation wrought by chemical injury. My unique and singular story speaks to the countless others in similar circumstances who cannot write theirs. As chemical disability becomes an epidemic all around the world, all of us victims deserve recognition and acknowledgement for our courageous struggle, and the tremendous inner strength and resourcefulness it takes for us to survive and endure in an unfriendly world, often completely on our own.

Most of the individuals who appear in my memoir have had their names changed to preserve their privacy.

INTRODUCTION

In the Beginning
1957-1977

My journey to silicone injury began in Lanciano, Italy. It is a small town in the Abruzzi region on the Adriatic coast. This is where I came into the world as Doralice De Pasqua on July 13, 1957. I grew up enjoying all the benefits that came with a large and close-knit family, a secure community, a definite cultural identity, a historical legacy, and time-honored values and traditions. My world was loving, accepting and safe. In other words, I had everything a child needs to thrive.

In 1968 however, I was quite suddenly uprooted from everything I knew and loved. My family and I left the small town of my birth and immigrated all the way to the United States. I knew instinctively that this wasn't good for me, and begging and crying, I asked my mother to leave me behind with my aunt. This particular aunt was childless and would have loved to have me. I was then at the tricky age of eleven, looking forward to my adolescence and the next stage of my development, and I longed to remain in this familiar, safe place.

Besides leaving our entire family behind, it ripped my heart apart to leave my school friends behind, all the girls I had been with from first to fifth grade in Mrs. Casalone's class. Ours was an all-girls elementary school, and we had occupied the same classroom for five years, so we were like a family. Although we would miss our teacher who had taught us every subject in the curriculum during those five years, we were all excited to be moving on and attending middle school in September. This was primarily because we would be sharing our classes with boys for the very first time. I was really looking forward to all the fun we would have as teenagers together. My best friend Maria, I, and the rest of our schoolmates fully expected to be lifelong friends and share all of life's milestones with each other. And Mrs. Casalone, we knew, would always be reassuringly close at hand, watching our progress all along the way, remaining available to us should we ever need her. This was the idyllic future I was anticipating. But it was not to be.

My family and I left from Naples on a cruise ship, and after seven days of travel arrived in New York Harbor. The moment I stepped onto the Port of New York I grew distraught. I was dismayed by how ugly and industrial everything looked, and how dirty and polluted the air smelled to me. I asked myself why we had left paradise to live in purgatory.

We settled in a suburb of Newark, New Jersey and began the long process of adjusting to American life. I'm sure this was a difficult and emotional process for my parents and sisters as well, but for me it was much more than that: it was honestly traumatic. Back then I was an extremely shy and sensitive little girl, and though this was fine within the confines of a protective, sheltered environment, once I was taken out of that environment I crumbled. No longer having my friends around, or all my cousins, aunts, uncles and grandparents, who liked me and cared for me, was devastating. Now it seemed no one liked me or accepted me, even though I was the same me as before.

In school I became very withdrawn, terrified of the American children making fun of me. I was labeled "foreigner" "corny" "bookworm" and "weirdo." This being the first time I'd been called such disparaging names, I felt completely bewildered. I didn't have a name for it then, but today this would be called bullying. My response was to make myself as invisible as possible and I succeeded. After a while I was ignored by the other kids and I ended up having no friends at all.

For seven years of my young life, from the sixth to the twelfth grades, I ate lunch alone. Often I would hide in the girls' bathroom and eat my lunch there. During recess I stood in a corner and watched the other children play and socialize. In class I sat at my desk day after day, mute and petrified, literally frozen in place, unable to reconcile the unfriendliness of my new world. It was a world I didn't belong to. I belonged back in Lanciano, enjoying the carefree, fun life that should have been mine. To this day there is no one in my family who knows the depth of the agony and pain I was feeling back then since there was no one whom I could confide in and no one who cared to listen. In my family it was expected that we always put on a brave front and deal with our problems on our own. It was impossible for us to discuss such things with each other. So I had no choice but to proceed along unsupported.

I did have one saving grace though—my intelligence. I was always an excellent student, always at the top of my class, despite the obvious language barrier. Studying and learning were two things I loved. I threw myself into them, trying to make them the anchors of my life. When I graduated high school as valedictorian of my class, I stood at the podium delivering the graduation address, but inside I was shaking, still feeling disconnected and disembodied. My mind had grown but the rest of me had been left behind. And my intellectual success felt hollow because socially I felt like an utter failure. I remained, in many ways, a traumatized eleven-year-old who had not been able to move forward. I had missed the adolescence that, as a young girl, I had been looking forward to so much. And this was true not just emotionally and psychologically but also physically. Although I had begun to menstruate at the usual age of thirteen, my breasts had never developed. I had not received the attention from boys, which I think is crucial at this age, and I had not been able to transition into adulthood in the way most of my classmates had. I continued to be invisible.

In college I finally came out of my shell and started being myself when I made friends with a group of Italian-American students, and found that I could at last relate to someone on a human level. None of these friends, however, were immigrants as I was, so I still couldn't process my painful immigrant experience with anyone. I was well into my forties when I finally managed to do so, aided by a series of professional counselors. In the meantime, I was an eighteen-year-old young woman who still felt like an eleven-year-old child in many ways. But I was expected to act like an adult. The only thing for me to do was fake it, and (happily or unhappily) I succeeded. I created a persona for myself that could competently deal with outside events, while on the inside I was desperately crying, longing to be normal, to be truly whole.

By the end of my sophomore year in college I made a decision. I could solve the issue of my flat chest, and so, in my mind, also solve the problems stemming from my missed adolescence. I would get breast implants. Now boys would notice me, I thought, and I would be able to get myself a boyfriend, gain confidence, and have a real social life. This, I believed, would allow me to catch up with everyone else. I would finally become the normal person I longed to be.

I went and did some research, and though the libraries only carried a couple of books about silicone gel breast implants, the authors' views were definite and unanimous—these medical devices were absolutely benign, safe and inert. And I was able to pay for them because my savings account had accumulated sufficient money from all the part-time jobs I had held since the age of fifteen. Still, my family was worried. They thought that operations of any kind were dangerous, and they asked me to reconsider. But I couldn't. I had already been cheated of my life once; I was not going to be cheated again! This seemed like the only way for me. My next step was to go to my gynecologist and tell her what I wanted to do. She referred me to a surgeon, and my surgery was scheduled for August 1977.

PART I
NEW JERSEY

1

Living with Implants
1977-1988

In life nothing ever turns out the way you expect. My decision to get breast implants had nothing to do with vanity. I saw it as a practical solution to a problem. The implants were supposed to fill the void in my body/ life, thus allowing me to live the normal life I wanted. But I soon learned things are just not that easy.

My breast implants surgery went well, and so did my recovery. Within a week I went back to school and started my junior year. I found it strange that none of my friends seemed to notice the change in my appearance, even though I went from a size 30-AAA to a 34-B. Did they really think that I grew a set of breasts over summer break? I'll never know because no one said a word. And that's the funny thing, I didn't get any kind of attention at all. I was finally "normal", and apparently normal does not warrant attention. Needless to say, I was disappointed.

The best thing about my implants was that now my clothes filled out very nicely, and I could wear all the fashions I loved. I even did a little modeling which was a lot of fun. Clothes, fashion and style were my passion from when I was very young. My mother tells me that at the age of two or three I would tell her which outfit I wanted to wear on any given day. I used to like to draw clothes for my Barbie dolls. And after I learned to sew, I started making my own clothes. At one time I considered going to design school, instead of college, to become a designer. But I chose college because there were other things I wanted to learn first. I figured I could always go to design school later.

The worst thing about my implants was that they were hard as rocks. Every six months or so I went back to my surgeon who would perform a closed capsulotomy, which is literally squeezing each breast to break the capsule the body forms around the implant. After having this done three or four times I stopped going, and just lived with hard breasts.

Although my implants did not transform my life the way I thought they would, my life nonetheless proceeded pretty normally over the next eleven years. I graduated college, finally had a boyfriend, got a job, travelled, went back to live in Italy for a while, changed jobs, made new friends. I worked hard at creating a happy, satisfying, fulfilling life. Nutrition was important to me and so was exercising and physical fitness. I was working in the fashion world looking forward to expanding onto an increasingly creative career path. I also looked forward to falling in love and getting married.

But I was plagued with seemingly minor and unrelated health problems which cropped up at irregular intervals.

One summer I developed and suffered with severe weed and grass allergies. A couple of years later it was the tree pollens that got me in the spring. Soon after I had recurrent and unexplained stomach problems, and was even tested for an ulcer. Then I developed an irregular heartbeat.

After coming back from vacation one spring, I went to the gym and did my regular work-out with weights. Instead of feeling energized as usual, my body hurt like never before and I was exhausted. This experience repeated each time I worked out and eventually I stopped going to the gym. I decided instead to walk and run in the park near my apartment after work every night. But my legs felt heavy and painful, and I felt worse instead of better from the exercise. I didn't know what to make of this. I figured I was simply overtired from my work schedule and my daily commute which was a total of three hours roundtrip on various buses, trains and subways. I didn't have time to pursue a better answer than that, and just gave up on physical exercise.

I also had recurrent back pain, sometimes severe, which once landed me in the emergency room. One time while I was living in Italy I felt very sick with pain in the liver area. I was taken to the hospital and was told it was just indigestion. But somehow I knew that wasn't quite right. Later on I developed an apparent bladder infection and was prescribed antibiotics: they made me sick and didn't clear up the irritation, which persisted for many months.

One time I was vacationing in Monte Carlo with a friend and was so tired and listless that I sat in a café for hours drinking cafés au lait, while my friend explored the city alone. Another time I was supposed to fly into Leonardo Da Vinci airport in Rome to meet up with the same friend, and together drive down the southern coast of Italy. I never made it because I was ill, and ended up leaving a message for my friend at the airport not to expect me.

Towards the end of 1986 I developed excruciating pain in the right side of my neck, shoulder, head and eye. No one could explain what it was and I was put on Tylenol with codeine for almost a year and sent for physical therapy. This particular symptom caused me to miss many days of work. After I had taken all my sick days my supervisor called me into his office and had a talk with me. He wanted to know why I couldn't manage this pain and show up for work every day. He held up as an example an employee in another department who had chronic back pain from an accident, but who would take his medication and come to work. I tried telling him that I didn't know the cause of my pain, that the medication wasn't very effective and that in fact it made me so woozy it simply compounded the problem. But he wasn't very interested in what I had to say and simply warned me not to take any more sick days.

All these maladies were baffling to me. Each time I went to the doctor with a new symptom, he would focus on that and forget about the others. There was no cohesive picture to suggest a diagnosis for a systemic problem. And without a diagnosis there was not much I could do except try to use mind over matter. Besides, my family got tired of hearing me complain each week when I went to Sunday dinner at my parents' house. I didn't look sick—I was the picture of health and beauty. And my mother's reaction was that everyone has aches and pains. She didn't seem to understand that mine were not ordinary aches and pains. And no one in my family seemed concerned at the variety and number of my symptoms. As usual, I was expected to buck up, push through, and put on a brave face. And I was certainly good at doing that—the persona I created in college served me well.

In 1988 I started feeling fatigued all the time. I had to literally push and drag myself everywhere. Every night after coming home from work, I would just collapse into bed. Every morning upon waking up I hoped to feel better, but as soon as I got up the horrible fatigue would still be there. And so I had to push and drag myself again, one more day. It felt like I had a heavy iron ball and chain attached to each ankle and each wrist, weighing and dragging me down.

That summer I was sent on a business trip to Tucson, Arizona. I spent four days in a beautiful hotel, away from my regular duties and routine, relaxing and enjoying myself. In that environment the fatigue was easier to bear. But as soon as I flew back home it hit me twice as hard. I thought maybe I picked up valley fever, a common infection from the desert, but I had not.

Then a peculiar new symptom started: a feeling of being constantly hot and overheated. This was peculiar for me because normally I felt cold and always wore suit jackets and sweaters in my very cool air conditioned office. Now I couldn't stand them and ripped them off.

At this time I was working in the marketing and advertising department of an international airline on Fifth Avenue in Manhattan, a couple of blocks away from Rockefeller Center. Everything about my job was glamorous—the location, the travel benefits, the people I dealt with. Although I loved the cachet of this job, it wasn't as creative as I wanted it to be. Through the years, as my symptoms multiplied, I became more dissatisfied with it, and contemplated making a change. I tried to figure out how to go to design school and/or find a more fulfilling occupation. But by summer 1988 it was all I could do to keep my head above water, and any desires or plans I had were put to the side.

One thing I had available to me that I enjoyed, and liked to make good use of, was the job perk of being able to fly practically anywhere in the world for free or nearly free. Even when not feeling well, I relished being in airports, on planes, in hotels and all kinds of new places. I felt that if I took a trip to de-stress and distract myself, perhaps I would feel better. So a work colleague and I decided to take an extra-long Labor Day weekend and fly down to Rio De Janeiro for some R&R. The trip started out well, but unfortunately it did not end that way. I became so sick that I actually spent the last day in my hotel bed. Back home I then spent the next three months battling a flu-like illness, and a renewed and much fiercer bladder infection.

My body completely broke down on December 28, 1988. I had just finished getting ready to go to work, and was about to drag myself towards the front door. Suddenly I experienced a crushing sense of exhaustion and I simply could not move anymore. Then it felt like a ton of bricks fell on top of me and I literally collapsed on the bed. I didn't get up again for four months.

2

CFS – Chronic Fatigue Syndrome
1989

On that fateful day December 28, 1988, my parents immediately came to get me and brought me to their home, where they could look after me. Thus began the journey for recovery, and the journey for answers, diagnoses, and understanding. What was wrong with me? My symptoms were severe and alarming. I had so much pain all over my body, I could hardly move. I was so exhausted I could barely get out of bed to go to the bathroom. The burning crushing pain in my chest was so bad it felt like a truck was sitting on it. My left arm was so weak, I couldn't use it at all. And my insomnia was so severe I couldn't get any rest. I had dizziness, headaches, weakness, nervousness, shakiness, gastrointestinal problems, pain in the liver and spleen areas, ringing in the ears, hair loss, swollen lymph nodes, a metallic taste in my mouth, sweats, chills, menstrual irregularities and continued bladder problems. My primary care physician gave me his verdict, which consisted of two diagnoses. The first was mononucleosis, an infectious disease caused by the Epstein-Barr virus which causes severe fatigue and can last for months. The second was pericarditis, inflammation of the lining of the heart.

I suffered and languished in bed, moaned and endured, day after day, week after week, month after month, in a stuporous state, racked by the torment of my symptoms and the fight going on inside my body. It was four months of sheer torture. By the end of April things finally started to calm down: I started emerging from the abyss. By May I was getting up and getting dressed every day and resuming some minor daily activities. The good news was that I was no longer bedridden; the bad news was that I still had a lot of symptoms. The more acute ones were gone. But I remained a broken person with chronic insomnia and sleep dysfunction, chronic debilitating fatigue and daily chronic muscle pain. The fatigue always worsened with exertion of any kind, no matter how minor. The use of any muscle anywhere in my body would bring on twitching, increased burning pain, and exhaustion.

As summer approached, I hoped to be nurtured and strengthened by heat and sunlight, my two favorite elements. But no matter how much time went by these symptoms would not resolve or improve. They were here to stay. It was as if these various functions and components of my body had been severely ratcheted down and locked into place into a much lower, faulty and defective level of functionality. Clearly, something more was wrong.

One night as I watched TV with my family, I saw a segment on a new illness called CFS or chronic fatigue syndrome. When the symptom list appeared on the screen, I shouted, "That's me! That's what I have!" I quickly located an infectious disease/immunology specialist who was already seeing CFS patients, and made an appointment. Soon enough, I was diagnosed with CFS, also known as CFIDS or chronic fatigue immune dysfunction syndrome. Originally thought to be caused by a virus, CFS is like an unresolved, never-ending mononucleosis, leaving its sufferers chronically fatigued, debilitated, and disabled for years, even for life.

Today the cause of CFS is still under investigation. Ongoing research centers on the roles of the brain, immune, endocrine, cardiovascular and autonomic nervous systems, as well as on genetic and environmental factors. CFS is characterized not only by unrelieved fatigue, which can be severe and causes a substantial reduction in daily activities, but also by unrefreshing sleep, postexertional malaise, muscle and joint pain, impairment in concentration and memory, headaches and hormonal imbalances. By the time I received my diagnosis I knew that I would never be the same again, that my life had changed forever. There had been a devastating downward shift in the state of my health, and there was no going back. What I had to do now was adapt and optimize.

There was, and still is, no cure for CFS, so the best one can do is try to alleviate symptoms. I couldn't use drugs because I didn't tolerate them. Antibiotics, anti-inflammatories and other pharmaceuticals prescribed for me caused unusual reactions and made me worse. So I had to take a different route. Instinctively I knew I had to rest a lot and pace myself throughout the day, and learn not to overexert myself. Common sense and my knowledge of nutrition told me to maximize my nutritional status by eating whole, nutrient-rich foods and taking supplements. And to minimize and relieve stress, I found myself drawn to relaxing activities such as strolling or sitting in nature, listening to music, and doing meditative exercises. Adopting these lifestyle changes allowed me to create a new balance, a new space within which to be. While not changing the symptoms, they brought me a certain stability, calm, and acceptance.

And this is where I found myself in the summer of 1989. The big event that summer was my sister's wedding in our hometown in Italy, where our entire family would be gathered. This was the first wedding among us five sisters, and for a while I thought I would have to forego it and remain home alone. Gratefully I was able to travel and join my family overseas for the joyous occasion. It was a delightful break after the horrific year I'd had, a memorable interlude.

We all had a wonderful time relaxing and sunbathing on the beautiful Adriatic beaches, shopping and bargaining at the outdoor markets, and gathering for delicious meals with family and old friends, while preparing for the wedding celebration which was to take place in early September. It had been years since my parents, my sisters and I had all been in Lanciano together, and it was just wonderful. But it would be the last time. It would also be the last time I flew on a commercial airline, the last time I would go overseas, and the last time I would attend one of my sisters' weddings.

3

Stabilization

After the wedding, life returned to its normal routine. Of course, for me it was a "new" normal: my job was gone, my apartment was gone, my healthy friends were gone. I was living with my parents again at the age of 32 and trying to come to terms with my new reality as a chronically ill person.

I joined CFS support groups and patient organizations. I worked with conventional as well as holistic doctors and alternative practitioners. And I researched anything and everything that I thought might be healing and restore a higher level of function to my body, especially in the field of natural medicine: herbs, homeopathy, nutritional treatments, detoxification protocols, mind-body connections, energy medicine, bodywork techniques, and many, many others. This became my new work, my new life.

As summer gave way to autumn and then winter, it became more difficult to hold onto the new balance I had created. Many of my symptoms waxed and waned, or worsened, and old ones started acting up again. Digestive and gastrointestinal disturbances reestablished themselves, and I started losing weight. I began to experience cerebral weakness and central nervous system distress, including nervousness, irritability, agitation, and moodiness. I couldn't understand why I was getting worse again since I was doing everything right. As my family can attest, I was very disciplined with my diet, my rest schedule, my treatments. Obviously what I was doing, though, wasn't good enough. So I kept searching, interviewing doctors, finding out about new treatments, talking to other CFS patients.

By the early part of 1990 I had lost 10 pounds, a significant amount for me, since I am 5'5" tall and normally 113 pounds. As my brain and central nervous system distress continued, I found myself getting more and more depressed as I was less and less able to cope. It appeared that my body was going through another breakdown. I had to fight it—I didn't want to end up bedridden again. New medical tests didn't reveal anything unusual. In desperation, I again tried drugs, but as before they did more harm than good, and I discontinued them. Then I found a new holistic doctor and started on her program of nutritional supplementation. This afforded me some minor relief, enough to keep me going and give me hope, but not enough to sustain and rebuild my broken-down body. After a few months I went to another alternative practitioner who, through an unorthodox method of testing, found an irregularity in my thyroid gland. Actually, he found numerous irregularities in various glands, organs, and tissues, and he prescribed remedies for all of them. The problem was that they were too many remedies for my body to process and metabolize, especially given the malabsorption syndrome I had developed. Eventually I would give up on all the remedies, except for the one that treated the thyroid, which my body really liked and needed and which made a somewhat noticeable difference.

At this point it was early 1991 and I had made it through another year without much progress and without recovering that balance that was so crucial. I want to note that at this time CFS was not well understood by anyone. All doctors, including the alternative and natural ones were just stabbing in the dark, targeting whatever they could in a hit-or-miss fashion. Finally, though, I learned of a doctor who had developed a comprehensive treatment program, addressing what he believed to be the various aspects of CFS. He was attracting CFS patients from all over the country. After reading about his protocols and then consulting with him, I decided to trust him and put myself through the program. This consisted of intravenous vitamin and mineral solutions to strengthen and build up the body (IV's); his own special formulation of supplements to address various symptoms and body systems; dietary restrictions and specific agents in order to clear parasites, candidiasis, and other opportunistic infections; allergy testing and treatment; chelation therapy for heavy metals; and biofeedback to retrain the nervous system. Fortunately I had been able to purchase extended health insurance coverage through my previous employer, which paid for practically all the treatments.

I started out with the IV's, supplements, and dietary restrictions. Within a few months I had regained all my weight, my brain and nervous system had calmed down and rebalanced, and my condition had stabilized. Going to this doctor's office two or three times a week and sitting in a roomful of patients taking IV's for three or four hours at a time became a social outlet for me. We chatted among ourselves and the staff, got to know each other, compared notes, witnessed each other's progress or lack thereof, and became a sort of impromptu support network. The doctor's wife even gave cooking classes. It was a healing, friendly, supportive environment—just what I needed.

By the summer I had been stable for several months and felt very grateful. I had had two very long years of struggle and distress, of coping and not coping so well. I had been on a desperate search, on a rollercoaster of hopelessness and hopefulness. Now maybe things would be better. In order to celebrate I wanted to get out of town, to go on vacation. I heard about a holistic lakeside resort in upstate New York, which offered organic food, massage, bonfire gatherings and sing-alongs, games, and spiritual classes. I signed up and got a CFS friend to join me, drive us up there, and share expenses. We met many interesting people there, including others with CFS who, like us, wanted to relax and rejuvenate in a beautiful, nurturing, and natural environment.

I was hoping that now I could solidify my progress and move forward into a deeper level of recovery. I knew that I had to live with CFS, but I wanted to live better.

After returning from my restful and fun vacation, I continued my treatments and started on the other parts of the program. Allergy testing revealed numerous allergies, most notably pollens, weeds, and grasses, but also some foods and other substances. I was immediately started on allergy shots. I also tested positive for heavy metals, and I was advised to begin chelation therapy. I was feeling overloaded by the allergy shots though, and I elected to wait. I had learned by now that my body couldn't handle too many treatments simultaneously. My body needed time to adjust to the shots and start responding to them positively. However, this never happened because I continued to feel overloaded and then sickened by them. My doctor guessed that I was reacting to the phenol preservative in the shots and discontinued them. My experience with chelation therapy, in this case a series of IV's of a synthetic substance called EDTA, was similar. I experienced negative brain reactions to it, and it was quickly discontinued. The last part of the program was biofeedback, which I tried on a few occasions, but with no success whatsoever.

These results from the second half of the program were highly disappointing and discouraging for me. If I was having reactions to treatments, how could I possibly be able to improve my symptoms? Why was I having reactions? What did this mean? Something else had been bothering me for a while as well: I had noticed a heightened sensitivity to perfumes and fragranced products. Was this related to my other reactions? What did it all mean? As a member of the American Academy of Environmental Medicine, my doctor was not unfamiliar with these reactions and sensitivities, but he didn't have any answers to my questions.

Once again, it was up to me to search for explanations and solutions.

4

The Truth Is Revealed

Since my collapse in 1988 I had entertained certain nagging thoughts and suspicions in the back of my mind about my breast implants. Each time I saw a new doctor or practitioner I was required to disclose my entire medical history, including the surgery, on the intake forms. As a proactive patient, a patient who takes charge of and responsibility for her part in the healthcare equation, I also made it a point to tell the doctor in person about the implants during the initial office visit, and to directly ask if he thought they were a factor in my condition. Without exception, all the doctors answered in the negative. Each time I felt that I had done my duty. Had they?

My massage therapist, whom I had met at the lakeside resort during the summer, was a very intuitive and perceptive woman. She often sensed energetic or emotional blockages in my body and worked to clear or shift them. During one of my massages she had a strong impression that my implants were not good for me, that they were hurting me, and she told me so. Since I had learned to trust her discernment, that was all I needed to hear. It was confirmation of what I already knew intuitively. I knew at that moment that all of the doctors were wrong and that I wanted those implants out of my body. Among the dozens of practitioners, doctors, and specialists of all stripes and persuasions, backgrounds and outlooks, training and experience, whom I had consulted, not one of them had considered, even for a moment, the role that breast implants could be playing in my very serious health problems. It took a psychic woman to know the truth.

Quite coincidentally—although it has become quite clear to me that there are no such things as coincidences, since everything in life is interconnected—a week or so later there was a news story on television about possible problems with breast implants and some California court cases in which women were suing their surgeons and implant manufacturers. At the end of the show the network placed a statement at the bottom of the screen asking viewers *not* to call in for additional information. I found this remarkable. Obviously, there was something big going on, yet they were keeping a lid on it! In those pre-internet days, I was desperate for more facts but couldn't get them. Within a few months though, the information on breast implants exploded.

After my massage therapist's revelation, I searched for a knowledgeable specialist to consult, and I ended up seeing a rheumatologist. Like all the others, he didn't think the implants were the cause of my symptoms, but he did think I had an additional condition that hadn't been diagnosed before: fibromyalgia or FM. This is a complex chronic disorder characterized primarily by widespread muscle pain and tender points. This was certainly good information to have as it explained the muscle pain I had experienced even before my collapse. Like CFS, fibromyalgia did not then, and does not now, have a cure, and because the two have a number of symptoms in common, such as sleep dysfunction, fatigue, headaches, and concentration problems, the conditions frequently overlap in patients. Like CFS, fibromyalgia was not well understood at the time. Today research points toward malfunctions and disregulations of the central nervous system as well as to genetics. Some even believe that CFS and fibromyalgia will turn out to be the same syndrome. Clearly the hallmark of fibromyalgia is pain; of CFS, exhaustion. I had them both, but this didn't answer the questions I had about my reactions and sensitivities, nor did it explain the role of my silicone breast implants. Still, it wouldn't be much longer before all was revealed.

Between the end of 1991 and the beginning of 1992 media reports on silicone breast implants started coming fast and furious. They were about the disclosures coming out at the trials. They were about the doctors who had connected women's illnesses to their breast implants. They were about the women's support groups spreading around the country. They were about the lawyers who were exhorting more injured women to come forward. They were about the repeated failures of the Food and Drug Administration to regulate and ensure the safety of implants. They were about the plastic surgeons who claimed that they only knew what the manufacturers told them. They were about a new debate, a new fight in the country, which would pit 400,000 injured women against very powerful companies.

Right away I did three things. One, I became a member of several women's support groups and ordered all the back issues of their newsletters in order to get up to speed on what had been happening the last few years. Two, I found a law firm that was handling implant cases, and I became a client. Three, I went back to my surgeon and scheduled the removal of my implants.

5

Explant
1992

The extent of what had been perpetrated by silicone implant manufacturers over the course of thirty years finally came to light when they were forced to disclose internal documents and memos at trial. These showed unequivocally that:

1) They knew that silicone is not inert. In fact, they had at one time considered developing it as an insecticide.

2) They were well aware that silicone implants bleed, leak, and rupture, but they did nothing about it.

3) The short-term animal testing that was conducted showed immune-system reactions, inflammatory responses, and migration of silicone gel.

4) They never conducted any long-term or lifetime studies to assess the long-term effects.

5) They were aware that women were getting sick.

Hundreds of thousands of women were duped, used as guinea pigs in their unofficial experiment. Many of these women developed devastating autoimmune diseases, which started out as vague aches and pains, fatigue, and flu-like symptoms. These slowly progressed to other, more serious, but seemingly unrelated or inconsistent problems such as numbness, headaches, abdominal pain, rashes, dry eyes, weakness, chest pains, memory loss, hair loss, severe muscle pain, joint pain, and balance problems. Finally they were diagnosed as atypical forms of connective tissue disease, arthritis, lupus, Sjögren's syndrome, scleroderma, and other rheumatic, systemic diseases that destroyed their bodies and their lives. The reason there was disbelief and controversy over this is that the women did not fit the definition of the standard forms of those diseases. This is what the implant manufacturers seized on and used in their campaign to discredit women and appear blameless in the public's eye. They refused to acknowledge a new syndrome caused by silicone poisoning, having various atypical manifestations. (I will note here that the same thing happened with Gulf War Illness. The US government refused to acknowledge the emergence of a new syndrome associated with various chemical exposures in veterans of the first Gulf War, 1990-1991.) But juries were not fooled. In the few cases that went to trial, they awarded women millions of dollars in damages.

At this point, my first priority was to get those toxic silicone bags out of my body. The surgery was scheduled for April, but when I presented my surgeon with a list of special requests, he had second thoughts. My reactions to chemicals and fragrances had gotten much worse, and I was extremely concerned about undergoing anesthesia and not surviving the surgery. I even tried to donate my body to science, in case I didn't make it. I contacted a nearby university hospital, where a rheumatologist was doing research. Unfortunately, his research was only on live subjects—he had no protocol for accepting cadavers, and so he couldn't accept my offer. My list of requests to the surgeon included less toxic anesthesia, limiting the number of drugs used during surgery (such as tranquilizers), glass bottles for IV fluids rather than plastic ones, and that the staff and personnel wear no fragrances. As he read the list, he became very nervous and agitated, and he asked my reasons for it. He decided that he could not accommodate me, and he cancelled the surgery. Now I was forced to find another surgeon, and I wasn't quite sure how to go about it.

My concern that I might have a horrible reaction to anesthesia that would either kill or maim me spurred me to do some research. Eventually I was referred to an anesthesiologist who used a method called paravertebral block. After speaking to him, I felt sufficiently reassured that his method would work and be safe for me. I asked that he refer me to a surgeon who would understand my concerns and be willing to work with me, and he did. My new surgeon was wonderful from the very beginning. He was completely open, understanding, and accepting, not only of my special requests, but also of the larger context of my illness and its relation to the implants. Many surgeons refuse women's requests for explantation, not because they make what they consider extraordinary demands as I did, but because they don't accept that the implants, which are key to their livelihood, are causing any problems. I felt very fortunate, peaceful, and taken care of by a surgeon who put his ego aside and focused on helping me.

My surgery took place in August 1992. My sister drove me to the hospital, where I felt nervous and apprehensive, even though I had complete confidence in both my surgeon and anesthesiologist, and in all the safeguards that had been put in place. This was a far cry from the way I'd felt in 1977, when I'd experienced nothing but calm assurance and positive expectation. My trepidation was about simply not knowing how my body would react, what the surgeon would find inside my chest, and what would happen afterward.

I woke up in the recovery room crying, and I continued to cry for quite a while, unable to stop. The nurse on duty told me that this was a reaction to the anesthesia. But I was alive. I had made it! The surgery went extremely well and smoothly. My surgeon was able to remove both implants and capsules intact. There was no visible silicone gel within the chest cavity, which was very lucky for me. Some women have so much silicone gel dispersed in their chests that it necessitates extensive scraping of muscle and tissue, and results in severe scarring and deformity. My right implant, though, did show signs of having ruptured at a much earlier date, evidenced by dense fibrous and scar tissue at that location. This was not much of a surprise to me because in May 1989, after I was no longer confined to my bed, I had found two lumps in my right breast. A mammography done at the time was reported as "normal", meaning "no cancer". A repeat mammography by my surgeon a year later indicated a "contour abnormality", which should have been entertained as a possible rupture, but was not. The lumps never changed in the intervening years because, by the time I discovered them, my body had completed the containment of the leak within those lumps. I believe that the rupture took place the first week of December 1988, three weeks before my collapse, when I felt a very strange pain sensation beneath my implants. Upon consulting my surgeon, I was told that nothing was wrong, and no mammography was ordered. I know now that the four months I spent in bed soon thereafter was the outward manifestation of the process my body went through as it was assaulted by the leaking silicone gel, attempted to deal with it, and then contained it.

It was a tremendous relief to no longer be carrying around two bags of toxic and dangerous chemicals. I had cleared the first hurdle. But what about the second hurdle? The recovery period still to come was a mystery.

6

The Correct Diagnosis

My attorney was a busy man, focused exclusively on the facts and legalities of the implant cases. In all the time I worked with him, I only met him once. To help guide and shepherd the women through the process, he had a female doctor on staff who was warm, caring, and sensitive. She was the one person who knew and understood all aspects of each case, the legal, the medical, and most important for the women, the emotional. She knew how difficult the legal battle was for us, and how devastating our medical histories were. And she also knew that not only our breasts and bodies had been ruined, but our lives as well. Our hopes and dreams had been shattered. Her presence in my life at that time was a tremendously calming and supportive influence. No matter how my case turned out, I would be forever grateful for her kindness, empathy, and assistance.

In preparing my case the most important thing we needed was the correct diagnosis. I was sent to see a rheumatologist who, by virtue of having seen and examined hundreds of women with implants and health issues, had become an expert in silicone-associated disease. I was excited. After wasting years on doctors who understood nothing about my situation, I would talk to a true authority. This knowledgeable doctor was able to connect all the dots and create a cohesive picture of what had happened to me.

When it received silicone breast implants, my body considered them foreign objects and immediately started walling them off from the rest of its biology by building a capsule around each one. Over time the capsules thickened and hardened and constricted the implants. At this point I went to my surgeon and complained, and he performed a closed capsulotomy to break the capsules and restore softness to the breasts. This allowed silicone gel, bleeding through the porous envelope of the implants, to escape into my body and start migrating to various destinations. As time went by my body repaired the broken capsules and proceeded to strengthen them and constrict them around the implants again. Then another closed capsulotomy was performed, and more silicone gel escaped and traveled into my body. This cycle was repeated several times until May 1981, when the last closed capsulotomy was performed. Approximately three months after that I started experiencing the first of my troublesome and puzzling symptoms—severe allergies.

So from 1977 to 1981 I was subjected to repeated seepage and escape of silicone gel into my body. The way my body dealt with this foreign invader was by mobilizing macrophages to digest and assimilate it. Macrophages are special cells of the immune system which break down infectious and toxic substances.

However, silicone cannot be digested like other substances. Nonetheless, the macrophages continued their unsuccessful attack on the gel since that's their job, which caused inflammation and chronic over-activation of the immune system. This chronic inflammatory and hyperactive state leads to autoimmunity, a condition where the body starts attacking and destroying itself. The appearance of my very first symptom, allergies, took a total of four years and repeated bouts of gel release because that's what it took to damage the system that handles incoming allergens. As the silicone gel continued to travel within my body, symptoms changed, jumped around, and progressed as more systems and organs were affected.

By December 1988 I had undergone more than eleven years of constant inflammation and hyper-reactivity and was in pretty bad shape. Then my implants ruptured and released a large amount of silicone gel, which completely overwhelmed my body. This led to my collapse, the subsequent four months spent in bed, and my emergence as a disabled person. Silicone gel travels to all parts of the body but has a particular affinity for muscles and other connective tissues. In the end, my diagnosis reflected this fact: inflammatory, systemic, atypical connective tissue disease due to chemical immunotoxicity.

7

MCS – Multiple Chemical Sensitivity

My search for explanations was finally over. I now knew what was wrong with me, I had the right diagnosis, and the implants were gone. My search for solutions, though, was another matter.

For several months after the surgery I felt worse: weaker, more fatigued, more debilitated, with exacerbation of all my symptoms. I continued to work with my CFS doctor, using those treatments that helped and strengthened me. My rheumatologist gave me his blessing for this since he had no alternatives to offer me. He understood that there was no cure for silicone poisoning, and he had also found, in his practice, that drugs and medications provoked adverse reactions in the injured women, and so he no longer prescribed them. All that remained for me was to wait and see the effects of the implant removal.

Some women got better after explantation, others made some improvement, and still others experienced no benefit. The deciding factors were the length of time the implants were in the body, whether there was a rupture or not, and the amounts of leakage and seepage.

My implants were in for 15 years, and I did have a rupture, a major leakage, and repeated bleedings. This didn't bode well, but I was still hopeful.

After many months my symptoms subsided to the same level that existed prior to the surgery. Now would come the real test. Would my body go beyond this baseline point?

One thing I noticed though was that my sensitivity and reactivity to perfumes, fragrances, and odors seemed to be worsening. It was no longer a matter of simply disliking the smells, or finding them extremely unpleasant to be around, or experiencing them as deeply magnified or amplified. It was now a matter of feeling sicker each time I encountered one. I couldn't stand my mother's Chanel No.5 perfume, so after much complaining and haggling, she finally agreed to leave it in the car and not use it in the house. I asked her to warn me every time she used nail polish remover so that I could remove myself to a different part of the house. Whenever she dusted the furniture with Lemon Pledge, I shut myself up in my bedroom. Eventually I had to find fragrance-free substitutes for many of the products we used daily, such as soap, dishwashing liquid, laundry detergent, shampoo, and moisturizing lotion. This proved a struggle since it was difficult for my mother to give up her favorite personal care items. The situation was the same with my sisters, who visited frequently. I couldn't blame them—no one wants to be dictated to regarding their personal choices. But I was constantly fighting against a barrage of smells and odors coming at me from all sides, overpowering me, knocking me down again and again. I had no control of my environment, no control of what my family did. So repeatedly I asked, pleaded, negotiated, and explained, trying to win compliance from my family, but it wasn't easy. I know my family accommodated me as well as they could under the circumstances. At least I had my own safe room to escape to. I spent most of my day there, and used the kitchen only during off hours. At one point I managed to appropriate another much larger bedroom, which was right next to mine, and this gave me, in essence, the whole second floor to myself. I kept it as fragrance-free and safe as was possible.

Hypersensitivity to fragrances, synthetics, and chemicals is a phenomenon called MCS, multiple chemical sensitivities or EI, environmental illness. The symptoms of this disorder are triggered by exposure to chemicals in the environment. These are not simple allergies. The mechanisms of MCS are still not understood, but they are very complex and involve the nervous, immune, and endocrine systems, genetic variations and impaired detoxification abilities. Many people with CFS and fibromyalgia also have MCS, which leads one to conclude that all three syndromes are probably related. In my case there is no doubt that exposure to chemicals from silicone breast implants caused the manifestation of all three of these syndromes.

Silicone gel contains dozens of harmful chemicals, many of which are neurotoxins. The following is only a partial list:

- Silicon—it accounts for approximately 45% of the gel.
- Silica—used as a filler, it has been known for decades to be deadly in the lungs.
- Aluminum—used as a catalyst in turning liquid silicone into gel. It is known to be toxic in the body.
- Platinum—also used as a catalyst and known to be toxic. The combination of platinum with the rest of the chemicals created a virtual chemotherapy drug.
- Benzene—known carcinogen derived from petroleum.
- Toluene—solvent derived from crude oil.
- Formaldehyde—toxic disinfectant and preservative.
- Polyvinyl chloride—known carcinogen.
- Phenol—corrosive, poisonous derivative of coal tar. Used as a preservative.
- Naphtha—solvent.
- Acetone—fragrant, flammable solvent.
- Cyanoacrylate—adhesive.
- Isopropyl alcohol—solvent.
- Freon—refrigerant.
- Epoxy resin—adhesive.
- Amine—ammonia derivative.
- Ethyleneoxide—flammable, toxic compound used as a sterilizer.
- Color pigments—release agents.
- Solder—catalyst and polymerizing agent.
- Antioxidant rubber—solvent and catalyst.

Exposure to these and other chemicals can also happen in other ways, including through the air we breathe, the water we drink, the foods we eat, the clothes we wear, the environments in which we live, work and play, and the many specialized products we use. When MCS develops, the most useful thing to do is practice avoidance. In my case, I could avoid external toxins, but I couldn't avoid internal ones, the ones inside my body. The next thing to do is to detoxify. This is considered the premier treatment.

I was in touch with a large number of silicone-injured women across the country, all of whom were going through the same ordeal as I was, but with individual variations. Some of them were trying various detoxification methods, with mixed or unclear results. Nine months after my surgery I realized I could no longer wait and see if my body would heal on its own: it was clear that it wouldn't; it was obvious that it needed help. It was time to try to detoxify the chemicals.

8

Detoxing and Dancing
1993

The health club was located in one of the nicest towns in the area. The atmosphere was friendly, relaxed, and very quiet during the day. I had chosen it because the sauna smelled safe to me, and was told practically no one ever used it. They gave me a very inexpensive short-term membership and I was all set. My plan was to complete one month of use, working my way up from a low temperature to the highest recommended. The idea was to overheat the body, mobilize the toxins out of their storage places in the fat cells, and sweat them out. This method of detox is used in environmental health clinics, none of which were convenient to get to or affordable for me. So instead I decided to replicate the program on my own, which worked out really well.

Every day I set out late in the morning with my gym bag, looking forward to my "Day at the Spa." This was so much better than going to a medical clinic full of sick people. I enjoyed being in a health environment where everyone assumed I was also healthy, and which reminded me of my own healthy past. It was a way to bring my healthy fantasy to life for a couple of hours.

The experience was very soothing and calming for me. Each day I had the sauna completely to myself, so I didn't have to worry about others' personal care products and fragrances and I could follow my program without interruptions or strange questions from anyone. I did meet up with people in the locker room, but there the conversation was casual. I had found the perfect place to do sauna detox, and it felt more like a mini-vacation to me than a treatment. I absolutely loved the high heat, it was a balm to my painful muscles, it got the circulation going, and increased my energy. As the days and weeks went by I was told to expect smelly, toxic chemicals to come out of my skin. I waited for this to happen, but by the end of the month, I was still waiting. At that point my brain had gone into overdrive from the excessive heat and I knew I was done.

It was a tremendous disappointment to know detox had not worked for me. I had pinned a lot of hope on it, feeling it was my last chance to get well or better, but it was clear my body didn't have the ability to release the chemicals because it was damaged beyond repair. My rheumatologist had shared with me his belief that I fit the category of women who don't get well after implant removal, and I had wanted very badly to prove him wrong. But he had been right. Now I felt not only sad and dejected, but also incredulous that after everything I had gone through, after the long search for answers and solutions, this is what it had come to. It didn't seem real. I just wanted to wake up from the nightmare and have everything go back to normal.

One side effect of the sauna therapy was over-stimulation of my brain which produced a certain amount of hyper, nervous energy. And there was modulation of my muscle pain. These two combined to actually help me feel better. Even though I knew this was only a temporary effect, I decided to make full use of it.

It was now summer again, my favorite time of year, a time that is forever imprinted in my DNA as vacation/fun time. As a child in Italy, summer was for playing outside all day with my sisters. Summer was for going to the beach. Summer was for traveling with my parents: at age five they took me to visit Greece; at age nine they took me and my sister on a tour of northern Italy. Summer was the reward for a year well spent studying earnestly and being good. As a teenager, summer was the time to return home to our Italy to visit with the family and friends we had left behind. Summer was particularly precious to me at that time because of the misery I was in during the school year in America.

In the summer of 1993 I was about to turn 36 and aside from my family, all I had left were my doctors and my support groups. I had lost my health, I had lost my job and my career. I had lost my glamorous life of travel. I had lost all my healthy friends. I had lost my ability and the prerogative to move about the world as I desired. I had lost a big chunk of my freedom. But there was one thing I hadn't lost because I had not had it to begin with: a partner in life. I didn't know how I was going to do it, but I really longed to find a love partner.

Many silicone-injured women lost their husbands and marriages because of the severity of their conditions. I wasn't in any different place than them, but I still wanted to give my heart to someone who would give his heart back to me. Call it an impossible dream, but by that time dreaming had become easier than doing, so I allowed myself to dream.

I learned about a series of nonsmoking dances for single people. Dancing had always been one of my passions. I could no longer indulge in it of course, as it was another one of my losses, but this didn't stop me. Every Friday night that summer I got dressed up and went to a dance. After resting up and taking care of myself all week, this was my chance to listen to upbeat and energizing music, watch people dance, socialize a little, and feel part of the world for a while. Of course I had to stay away from the women with their perfumes, hair products, and scented body lotions, but the men were mostly OK. Talking to them was a very delicate undertaking because I couldn't tell them I was disabled, so I concentrated on finding out who they were and what they were looking for. It was an interesting experiment, the result of which was predictable: healthy men want healthy women.

Unavoidably at some point, I did have to talk about my problems in some manner, so I settled on telling people I had allergies, which everyone understood and accepted. Soon I met a man who was sympathetic to my plight because he himself didn't like fragrances! He wasn't sickened by them, he just liked things natural and appreciated a woman without make-up, hairspray, or scented deodorant. We went out for several weeks, he accommodating me by letting me choose the venues for our dates so I could protect myself. We liked each other enough, and enjoyed each other's company, but it soon became apparent that I could never keep up with him, and that if he ever understood the full extent of my condition, he wouldn't stick around.

Maybe what I should look for was not a healthy man, but one with a corresponding or similar chronic illness. In my various support groups, there were some male members, but the vast majority of patients with CFS, FM, MCS, and rheumatic diseases are women. I knew I was at a disadvantage, yet I couldn't see myself living the rest of my life disabled and alone. What was I going to do? I had no idea, but summer was coming to an end, and so was my short-lived hyper physical state which had carried me through the dances and the dates.

Having so much on my mind about my future, I felt myself going inward to contemplate all the imponderables of life and death, health and disease, love and family, success and failure, peace and suffering. What kind of life was I going to have? And what was the meaning of that life?

9

Spiritual Healing

After my youngest sisters left home, I took over their large bedroom and made it into my study. Besides having less of a fight on my hands now, and having to deal only with my mother and father on a daily basis, which gave me a greater measure of chemical safety and greater control over my environment, I could spread out more comfortably with all my books, papers, files, newsletters and correspondence. A certain peace descended upon me, and my life took on a different rhythm as I shifted from an outward focus to an interior one. I felt I had done all I could for my physical healing, now I wanted to turn to spiritual healing.

I created an altar in my new space, where I could meditate and pray, where I could center myself and allow spirit to fill me, and ask God to tell me His/Her will. I set up my altar on the round kitchen table from my old apartment, in front of a sunny window. The objects I used represented the elemental and spiritual forces that were meaningful to me: a brilliant crystal for earth, a soft feather for air, a red tapered candle, which I never lit, for fire, a lovely glass bottle for holding water, and a picture of Jesus Christ victorious in the spiritual realm, not crucified on the cross. From time to time I would add other devotional objects as they came into my life, such as rosary or mala beads, pictures of spiritual masters, special stones or statuettes, or candles of different colors. This altar became my refuge and my peace, the place where I was most happy, and I spent every afternoon there.

I started reading and studying more spiritual and metaphysical books. When I went into bookstores, I was drawn to the spiritual section, and particular books seemed to call out to me, and when I picked them up I could feel their energies in my hands. At home they would become part of my afternoon ritual at my altar. I had studied spirituality since college. By my early 20s I knew that no religion was right for me. I grew up in a Catholic family in a Catholic culture, so I am very deeply rooted in Christian values, morals and ethics. But the Catholic theology never made any sense to me, nor did it inspire the sublime feelings I expected and wanted from communion with God. I soon learned I felt the same way about other religions. With my solid Christian foundation, I knew I didn't need a church because I could find the kingdom of God and the Christ consciousness within, which is what Jesus' teachings are truly all about.

Now I was accessing that Christ consciousness daily, communing with the divine and deepening my connection. And I was asking for so many things that I needed: healing, if it was God's will; hope for that possibility; equanimity to deal with my symptoms and reactions; strength to face the daily struggles; patience with those who didn't understand or support me; guidance to direct my aspirations; comprehension of the significance of my experience; faith that no matter what, everything would be OK; and most of all sustenance from God's grace.

My spiritual teachers, inspirational guides and companions in this daily journey of mine which was to last several years, were the remarkable men and women whose wise and insightful words I was reading each day: Joel Goldstein, Emmet Fox, Catherine Ponder, Paramahansa Yogananda, Wayne Dyer, Carolyn Myss, Edgar Cayce, Gary Zukav, the Dalai Lama, Thich Nhat Hanh and many others.

At the same time I craved companionship with like-minded flesh and blood people, so I started making forays into events such as metaphysical lectures, discussion groups, classes and social get-togethers. Then I found a new, non-traditional church called Johrei, whose main practice is the transmission of spiritual light. It felt heaven-sent and appealed to me immensely. I joined, studied with the pastor, and started practicing with the other members. Unfortunately the church building, especially the Johrei transmission room, was rather toxic and I had a difficult time there, and reluctantly had to stop going.

My study continued and expanded into all areas of spiritual, energetic and vibrational healing. I didn't know if this kind of healing could affect the physical ravages in my body, but I wanted to believe it could. There were reports of miracle cures resulting from it. Since I had nothing to lose, I immersed myself in learning various systems and practices. This gave me a lot of solace, and a sort of supernatural hope that maybe one day all my efforts would pay off and I would be granted one of those miracle cures.

One of the most important parts of the work I was doing came with my discovery of the world of crystals. This fascinating world started calling out to me one stone at a time. Being a visual person who relishes beauty in all its manifestations, I found myself drawn more and more to the unique exquisiteness of rock, stone and crystal formations. The extravagant array and variety of these is staggering: a multitude of shapes, forms, structures, weights, densities, consistencies, textures, hues, tones, shades, color combinations, luminosities, transparencies, patinas, intricacies, patterns and designs, an explosion of beauty and creativity that touched my whole being. In the stores I felt an irresistible pull towards them and invariably found special ones that I couldn't leave behind, that I just had to buy and take home with me. One time I got the idea to go to a particular gift shop quite far from my house. I didn't need to buy a gift, so I didn't know why I got that idea. But I decided to go ahead and take a ride, get out of the house for a bit, maybe distract myself for a while. When I arrived at the gift shop, there it was in the window: a gorgeous, gleaming, luminous white apophyllite. I felt indescribably ecstatic to see it! It was like the universe was reuniting me with something precious. That apophyllite took up a special place on my altar generating and transmitting joy and happiness to me and my space. The physical beauty of crystals is breathtaking enough, but the light and energy they project is even more profound. This is why there is such a thing as crystal healing.

I started going to mineral and gem shows regularly to find the exotic specimens I was reading and learning about. I wanted to collect them all and surround myself with their beautiful, healing, uplifting energies and immerse myself in them. In time my study was full of them and was transformed into a healing chamber, where I felt myself bathed in their intense, penetrating and beneficent light. Those crystals and stones were conduits of the highest emanations of spirit. I felt so close to them, they were like friends, or like pets who give unconditional love and acceptance. And I loved them all the more because they were nontoxic: no fragrances, no noxious ingredients. Just pure earth and spirit. What a special gift!

Within the embrace of this special environment, I started dreaming and gestating my future. I had no idea what was possible, but it felt wonderful to be led in such an effortless way.

10

Money Matters

In 1990 I had applied for Social Security Disability Insurance (SSDI) with the diagnosis of CFS. My application went through the usual process, which meant an initial denial from the Social Security Administration (SSA). After I made an appeal, which was also denied, I hired a disability lawyer who prepared me to go in front of a judge to plead my case. When that day came the judge was very sympathetic. He believed I was disabled, and told me he wanted to approve my claim, but he needed a legal basis on which to do so. Since CFS was not recognized as a legal disability at that time, I needed different medical documentation. So for the first time since my ordeal began, I went to a psychologist to get an evaluation. This felt very strange to me because I felt like the sanest person on the planet. I was holding it all together in the face of an overwhelming and bewildering medical picture. How would this psychologist ever find me mentally ill? Remarkably he did. He took all my physical symptoms and ascribed them to psychological causes. This of course was normal procedure in the 1990s for CFS. Many CFS patients objected to this on the grounds that it would mark them for life and ruin any chances for future employment. I didn't care about that because I knew I could never work again. Incredibly the psychologist did not mark me for life. He said I suffered from a temporary somatoform disorder which he believed would resolve in two years. I must have really impressed him with my reasonableness, levelheadedness, and normalcy. But how I wished I could have made his pronouncement come true!

Nonetheless his report was sufficient to qualify me for disability and my claim was finally approved. The entire process had taken more than a year, but it was over and done with, and now I had a measure of security. Being approved for SSDI also made me eligible for Medicare which was a good thing because the extended health insurance coverage from my old job was about to run out.

Of course living with my parents was a tremendous help financially as I didn't have any overhead expenses. But once I got SSDI I started giving them a little something for rent, even though they never asked for it, because I didn't want to take advantage of their generosity. I also wanted to remain responsible and pull my own weight, and not allow disability to destroy what I still had left of myself. I needed to preserve my independent habits and continue being an adult, not backtrack into a dependent or childish role, which is a very alluring notion when one is quite debilitated and one's environment is conducive to it.

This was in 1991 when I was still figuring things out about my illness. By 1992 everything had changed dramatically. Financially I was looking at the possibility of a huge payout from the implant manufacturer if and when I went to trial and won. This is what I was preparing for, this was the payback I wanted for what had been done to my body without my informed consent. But I was concerned that I would not be able to withstand the rigors of a trial. Going to trial meant being in court every day, sitting up in a chair for eight hours, listening attentively to complex medical and obfuscating legal testimony, and being surrounded by dozens of people wearing numerous fragrances and chemicals, without being able to lie down and rest whenever I needed to, or go outside to get away from the odors and clear my head in the fresh air, or walk out and go home when I reached my limit. I was afraid it would break me down. I talked to my lawyer about this and he didn't like what he was hearing. He wanted me to be tough, and enthusiastic about going to trial. Didn't he know that my mind was willing, but my body was weak?

I tried thinking of things I could do to get me through the ordeal. Someone suggested I wear a personal air purifier around my neck to clean the air around me. Better yet, maybe an oxygen tank to keep my brain clear would serve double duty as a physical sign of my distress and disability. Unlike many other injured women, I did not look sick. I had no outward signs to signal to the world and to the jury the destruction and suffering I lived with. I could also wear a mask over my nose and mouth, like many MCS people do, to filter out odors and toxins. But this is not very effective, as chemical emanations can also be absorbed through the skin, eyes, and hair. And what about my fatigue and muscle pain?

Maybe the judge would allow me to bring in a cot to lie on. But even if I did all these things, I still would not have enough protection and safeguards.

On April 16, 1992 after mounting pressure, the Food and Drug Administration (FDA) suspended the production and sale of silicone gel breast implants until such a time that they could be proven safe. Saline-filled implants were allowed to remain on the market, even though they were responsible for injuries in some women. One of them was a friend of mine who ended up in a wheelchair due to nerve damage. Now that the FDA had finally acted, everyone's attention could be turned to the legal drama that was about to unfold.

Across the country 400,000 women and their lawyers were contemplating their payouts and their day in court. Implant manufacturers were contemplating the possibility of going bankrupt, and were very busy manipulating public opinion, the medical and scientific communities, and the legal system. And courts were contemplating the logistics of handling such a large number of cases. Plastic surgeons were not part of this debacle because although they profited from breast implant surgeries, they were not ultimately responsible for the product, the manufacturers were. Eventually, as is usually the case in situations of this magnitude, it was agreed that the best course of action was to combine the individual cases into one class action suit in a multi-district litigation. A class action suit would obviate enduring a trial, putting my worries to rest. It would also spare me from having my character attacked in court. But would it provide enough compensation?

Class action suits tend to be good for the defendants, the parties being sued, and for the attorneys, but not so good for the plaintiffs, the injured parties.

All of a sudden I had to revise my conception of the outcome. It wouldn't be millions of dollars. Maybe it would be hundreds of thousands of dollars, maybe less. This remained undecided and uncertain while negotiations between all parties proceeded, became arduous and protracted, broke down, started again, and continued for several years. At one point a multi-billion dollar global settlement was announced with a compensation grid covering all women according to levels of injury. The manufacturers were not admitting culpability nor acknowledging the link between silicone and disease. They had been successful in evading jury trials and were now going to discharge their responsibilities very cheaply. The women at the lower rungs of the grid, who were the majority, were not happy. The grid was based on traditional definitions of diseases, not atypical ones, so that it was virtually impossible to quality for the highest rungs. A big chunk of the settlement was going to administrative expenses, which were extensive. All in all it was a rather unsatisfactory ending to years of waiting and hoping for just compensation, but pretty typical for a class action suit. Then abruptly one of the manufacturers declared bankruptcy and the whole settlement fell apart.

We were back at square one.

11

Daily Life
1993-1996

Between 1993 and 1996 my psyche was dominated by the spiritual work that sustained me and elevated me above the fray. But the rest of me still had to handle the dilemmas of daily life with chemical injury.

As long as I followed my measured and slow routine, as long as I rested and recovered from each physical activity, as long as I avoided chemicals and fragrances, I could get through the day. This required control over my schedule and environment, which I didn't always have. The most trying times were holidays, special occasions and anytime visitors were at the house. Holidays meant my mother spent a lot of time in the kitchen preparing culinary feasts, restricting access to my own cooking. It also meant family would gather at our house bringing noise, odors and chemicals. I certainly enjoyed the celebrations, but they always wore me out. As time went on and I became more chemically reactive, I had to cut short my participation in these events and retreat to my bedroom more often.

Several times we had family visiting from Italy, staying with us for weeks at a time. It was a treat to see them and spend time with them, but exhausting and overstimulating for me on all levels. I was glad when everyone would go out, so I could have the house to myself.

Family milestones were another problem. The expectation was always that I would participate, and at first I did. I was able to attend my youngest sister's college graduation and another sister's graduation from nursing school. But later on I was too chemically sensitive to attend either of their weddings. In the end I missed out on many family functions, partaking of them only through photographs and videos.

At one point certain cooking odors started driving me crazy. And I noticed that the gas stove was affecting me adversely. To get away from all the activity and problems at the house, I would occasionally go to a movie theatre for a matinee where I was sure to encounter very few people. My favorite place to escape, however, was the beautiful park in the next town, where I could enjoy the clean air, the lovely green scenery, the duck pond, and the peace of nature.

I was still going to my CFS doctor's office at times to get IVs, but only until my veins started hurting and burning and could no longer tolerate them. The same thing happened with some of the supplements. I scrambled to find new ones my body could accept, a procedure I would repeat countless times over the ensuing years, as my body gradually lost tolerance to each new product.

Grocery shopping was impossible for me. Luckily my parents handled that when they did their own. All I could do was go into a store for a few minutes at a time, and pick up an item or two. If I had to go to a department store or walk through a mall, I always carried a small folding stool so I could sit and rest when needed.

As the smells in stores became more overpowering and sickening for me, I tried wearing a cotton mask, which turned out to be completely useless. So I adapted it to fit snugly and securely over my nose only and added more cotton to completely block breathing. This prevented fumes from directly reaching my brain. I called this contraption my "Miss Piggy Nose" because it resembled a pig snout. People stared at it but never said anything. I just assumed they thought I had had nose surgery, so I was never very self-conscious about it. I had tried wearing swimmers' nose plugs, but they didn't hold a candle to my Miss Piggy Nose.

All physical activity was excruciating and exhausting for me, yet I knew the importance of movement. At the park, or around the block, I would take a short walk to give my body the benefits of deep breathing, fresh air, increased circulation, and improved digestion. I could never do more than 20 minutes, but no matter how little or how much I did, I would arrive home drained, aching and throbbing all over, especially in my legs. The recovery period could last as much as an hour, lying in bed quietly, waiting for the twitching and inflammation in my legs to calm down, and for some of my energy to return.

Cooking, washing dishes, driving, shopping, walking, bathing, washing my hair, and any other sustained household chore debilitated me and required a mandatory rest and recovery period of varying length. I spent countless hours in bed crashing, collapsing, recouping, and listening to music, meditations, radio programs, and reading books.

Along with physical exhaustion and mental fatigue, there was the mental pressure of constantly dealing with the logistics and limitations of pain, loss of energy, and reactions to chemicals. Watching certain TV shows helped defuse this pressure. The Oprah Show was particularly good because it often affected my emotions and provided a catharsis, taking the focus away from my weary mind. Mystery novels had a similar effect on me because they shunted my mental processes to a different channel, and in the end the mystery was always resolved, unlike my symptoms. In 1995 the real life mystery of the O.J. Simpson trial provided me with months of distraction and release.

Sometimes, despite my best efforts, I was caught completely unawares by unexpected conditions. One night, after my parents were done in the kitchen, I was on my way downstairs to have dinner when I smelled acetone, and immediately ran back to my bedroom. I called out to my mother to let me know as soon as she was finished removing her nail polish. She did so and I went to the kitchen, but I continued to smell a strong odor of acetone even though the bottle was capped, and the soaked cotton balls were outside in the trash. As I frantically tried to find the source of the smell, I had a neurological reaction which triggered a crying jag. My mother finally told me she had spilled some on the floor, and had dried it with a tissue. That was it: the residue was enough to cause a major brain reaction. I put on gloves and a mask, got on my hands and knees and while sobbing, scrubbed that spot until all traces were gone. That incident left me sapped and shaken. I had never felt so vulnerable, powerless and out of control.

All the difficulties, disruptions, and pressures I faced at the house pointed to the fact that I needed my own place to live. Yet this didn't seem feasible. I couldn't live alone; I needed the help and support of my family. For now I would just have to continue making the best of the situation.

12

The Goddess Room

We had lived at the house since 1970. My sisters and I had all grown up there. For a chemically sensitive person it was an ideal house: everything in it was old and outgassed, no chemical vapors emanating from anything anymore. The carpeting was more than 30 years old. The linoleum floors were original to the house, as were the kitchen cabinets. The hot water baseboard heating system was completely nontoxic. And all our furniture had been with us for decades. From this perspective I felt very lucky compared to many MCS people who lived in toxic apartment buildings and newer houses. But the house didn't belong to me and ultimately I had no say in what would happen to it. My parents had wanted to remodel and update it for a long time. I had already dissuaded them from replacing the kitchen cabinets and renovating the bathroom, projects that I felt were too dangerous for me. But I had agreed to external painting and putting in a ceramic tile floor in the kitchen, both of which I had no problem with. Now they were adamant they wanted to replace the floors and paint the rooms on the second floor. I was very upset about this, but I couldn't get them to change their minds. They did agree to leave my bedroom alone: it was my private oasis, and they respected that.

In the end the solution was that I would stay at my sister's condo while the work was being done. I looked forward to spending time with my sister. However, she worked two jobs and was hardly ever home, and I ended up feeling very lonely. The condo was very small, so I had only brought the minimal essentials with me. I missed my books, my crystals, my altar, all the things that gave my life a sense of comfort, and I couldn't wait to get back to the house. But I knew I couldn't get back too soon or I would run the risk of having bad reactions and getting very sick.

Two months later I finally went home and I was impressed with the results. The smell of the paint and flooring had dissipated enough that I hoped I would be OK. I experienced no overt reactions. The upstairs looked beautiful and it inspired me to delve into one of my passions: redecorating my study and turning it into a special space. My creativity went into high gear and a vision came to me of a "Goddess Room," sparked by a calendar I had received as a Christmas present depicting gorgeous paintings of various mythical goddesses. I threw myself joyfully into my project, ecstatic to be creating again and to be involved in an endeavor that had a concrete, definite outcome, in contradistinction to my health and my life which didn't.

My study was large enough that I was able to redesign the floor plan to include several unique areas: a sleeping area, a study area, a living room area, an altar area, and a display area for my stones and crystals. I wanted it to be like my very own mini-apartment. My plan was to recycle and reuse as many things as possible, to cut down on the introduction of new items which could be problematic. My parents happily encouraged me to scavenge in the attic and the basement and make full use of whatever I found. What I found was a treasure trove of pillows, picture frames, decorative items, old pieces of furniture, costume jewelry, trinkets, fabrics, practically anything I might need. I set to work to clean, restore, and renew some of the items, and to take apart, redesign, and refashion some of the others. I sewed beautiful window treatments and pillow covers. I created a collection of framed goddess pictures that I hung on all the walls to unify the space and anchor the theme. And I worked with the principles of feng shui to ensure a harmonious flow of energy and an auspicious ambiance. Upon completion the room was magnificent. I loved it! And I had had so much fun creating it!

My goddess room wasn't merely an aesthetic upliftment for me, it went much deeper than that, as each goddess embodies different divine qualities, attributes, and strengths. Thus each depiction infused my room with a special, unique energy, contributing to and magnifying its healing power. As I spent time surrounded by these, I could feel them activating the corresponding energies within me, slowly unfurling from my own core, where they had lain dormant for a long time, spinning out, expanding out to fill my body, my mind, my heart, rising to the surface of my being, meeting my conscious awareness at a place of recognition and reunion. Now I could acknowledge

them as mine, I could take ownership of them. I needed
these recovered attributes to help me navigate the
increasingly choppy waters of chemical injury. Dealing
with progressive chronic disease, especially the gradual
advancement and exacerbation of MCS symptoms
requires extraordinary resources foreign to normal life.
Chemical injury is indeed alien territory. There is no
map to follow. I had to create my own. And that's what
the infusion of goddess energy helped me to do. As my
spiritual work continued, I developed the confidence
and boldness to formulate a grand plan for my future.

I started dreaming of my own house, a peaceful,
quiet, fragrance-free environment where I could control
all the variables and be safe, calm and undisturbed. The
best house for me would be one similar to my parents'
in a comparable neighborhood where the neighbors are
not fastidious about their yards and don't use pesticides.
At first I drove around various neighborhoods nearby,
checking out the construction and age of homes, the
conditions of lawns and yards, the amount of traffic
and congestion, and other features that would impact
my health. I felt I needed to remain close enough to my
family so they could continue to physically help me. The
real estate prices however were very high. And somehow
none of the conditions, situations, and neighborhoods
felt right to me. This wasn't going to work. What I
needed to do was get clear on exactly what I wanted for
myself, in spite of all my limitations, perceived and real.
I needed to dream my highest dream, and so I did.

I had always wanted to live in a warm climate and
get away from the New Jersey winters. I did especially

well with dry heat, as evidenced by my positive experience with the sauna. I even loved tanning beds for the same reason. It is a known fact that people with rheumatic diseases feel better in warm, dry environments.

In the mid 1980s I had visited Arizona and had fallen in love with it. It wasn't just the sunny desert climate I liked, it was also the native Indian influences and the spiritual vibrations that attracted me. I just knew that one day I would return to live there. Now I was reading about MCS people relocating to Arizona and other places in the southwest to escape their polluted and toxic cities, build their own safe houses, and congregate into small communities. That's what I wanted!

But how was I to achieve it? First of all, if I mentioned any of this to my family, they would think I was crazy. I could not expect any assistance from them. They all had their lives to lead and could not take time out to cater to a crazy dream of mine. Family can only do so much for you, after which point you become a burden and a bother.

Secondly, chronically ill individuals with serious and debilitating diseases are very lucky if they happen to have a devoted spouse or partner who can facilitate their interface with the world. The ones I have known have been able to achieve and accomplish much due to that special support. Obviously I didn't have that kind of relationship.

Thirdly, finances were an important consideration. A lot would depend on the outcome of the class action suit. I was hoping to receive a substantial amount that would give me the freedom to carry out my fantastic plans, but this was now in limbo.

All these factors contributed to a sense of impossibility. How could I possibly get to Arizona by myself in my condition? How could I possibly build an environmentally safe house by myself? How could I possibly live on my own in a faraway state? If I thought about it in practical terms, it was overwhelming. It was much easier if I thought about it in magical terms, knowing that if it was meant to happen, the universe would arrange it. So I visualized my little home in the Arizona desert, and I imagined my partner standing next to me, supporting me, helping me, doing what I couldn't do. And I saw us surrounded by a community of friendly, caring MCS people, all working together to maintain a social network as well as environmental and chemical safety against the onslaught of the outside world. I understood that these visions and messages were to be respected, that the universe was to be trusted, that it was working through me to fulfill my destiny as well as its own. This wasn't the time to take action, this was the time to incubate the dream. This was a time of magic, hope, excitement, expectations, grand plans, dreams, a revamping of my life in the works!

It was also a revamping of my very being: my spirit had been fortified and invigorated. I was a new person, transformed. To mark this transformation, I was led to become ordained in a nondenominational metaphysical church, a church with no building or dogma, just a collection of individuals who felt called to acknowledge and affirm their identities as spiritual beings having physical experiences on earth. Although I still didn't know the meaning of my physical experience on earth, the message was crystal clear: I was much more than a broken-down body. I had a spiritual self that was larger than my body and my illness. And my spiritual identity was not only undiminished by my extremely trying physical experience, it was actually activated and exalted by it. My physical life had a higher purpose.

This was an answer to my prayers.

I had been granted awareness of a higher sphere of life. I understood that no matter what happened on the physical level, from now on I would be carried by the spiritual realm. To resonate more closely with this realm I was led to choose a new name for myself, my spiritual name. And so I did. Through my meditation sessions at my altar I received the name that vibrates throughout the various levels, layers, dimensions and parts of who I am, of my total being. The name is long and difficult to pronounce—it reflects the complexities and difficulties within me. But it is also alliterative and rhyming, reflective of the harmony and flow that are also within me. After getting comfortable with my new name, I made it official and had it legally changed.

Now that I was in congruence and attunement with my higher self, my dream expanded even more: I saw myself living in a community of like-minded and like-awakened individuals. Surely, if I had had this kind of awakening, I expected that many other sufferers in the chemical injury community had also, and they would be looking for their spiritual family as well. What we could create together seemed boundless to me.

Thus I found myself at this culmination point of my journey. The journey was certainly not over. I knew it would continue, and reveal more wonderments and marvels. What I couldn't possibly know or imagine was how it would all play out.

13

Descent into Hell
1997-1999

I didn't attribute what happened to me at the time to the new paint and vinyl floor tiles. In retrospect, however, it is clear that the constant low-level exposure created low-level reactions inside my body, which over time crescendoed to intolerable levels, and dangerously aggravated my predicament.

It started while I was still working on my goddess room. I thought I was overdoing it, but even after completing the project and allowing myself complete rest, I continued to struggle and spiral downward. From 1997 to 1999 it was a gradual decline into desperation.

My symptoms spiked, they intensified, they clobbered me, they tightened their noose around me, they imprisoned me more and more. The quality of my life dissolved. I didn't know what to do.

I heard a doctor speak on the radio and decided to go see him. My mother drove me to his office on Long Island, a two-hour, one-way trip which required passing through the middle of Manhattan. For five years I had commuted into Manhattan to my airline job on Fifth Avenue. I was way too sick to miss my job, but I now felt excited to be back in my old milieu, even just in passing, to experience the throngs of people in constant motion, the gridlocked traffic and the bike messengers weaving in and out of it, the multitude of store display windows, the skyscrapers casting shadows everywhere, the street vendors peddling their wares, the men and women in business suits and other fashionable attire, the wonderful architecture, and the different ethnicities contributing to the color, diversity, dynamism, fast pace and sophistication of this city I loved.

But my excitement was quickly quelled by the fact that I couldn't breathe. The heavy traffic fumes were seeping into our car. My nose and brain were engulfed in a cloud of hydrocarbons. The smell was overpowering. I felt trapped. My brain was fading, weakening, going into a hypoxic state. I needed oxygen. It took an agonizing half hour to get across town to the Midtown Tunnel. As soon as we emerged on the other side, I felt an immediate decline in the level of pollution in the air quality. My brain had become so exquisitely sensitive that I was now a human barometer.

I asked the new doctor to prescribe oxygen for me and he wouldn't do it. Instead he prepared a homeopathic remedy for gasoline and told me this would protect me in traffic. I was very dubious, but I decided to try it for the ride back home. Within minutes of ingesting the drops I had a major brain reaction: I felt poisoned, like someone had injected gasoline directly into my brain causing disorientation, confusion, fogginess, restlessness, irritability, anxiety, and panic. I cried all the way home, my body's automatic response to wash out the poison.

Homeopathic remedies contain minute amounts of substances diluted in water. The idea, similar to that behind vaccines and allergy shots, is to stimulate the immune system to respond, and create resistance to the offending substance. This is a nice theory, but it doesn't work against neurological mechanisms or autoimmune disease. When you're chemically poisoned, introducing one more chemical into the body, no matter how diluted, pushes you over the edge. A trace, a molecule is all it takes.

Medicare only reimburses for home use of oxygen for very specific, life-threatening respiratory and cardiopulmonary diseases. Basically you have to be dying to get oxygen. How could I explain that my brain was dying of chemical intoxication? After making it clear that I would pay for it out of my own pocket, one of my other doctors wrote me a prescription, and I started receiving weekly delivery of oxygen tanks at home. Because I didn't tolerate the standard plastic cannula and tubing, I ordered a ceramic mask and stainless steel tubing from the Environmental Health Center in Dallas, TX. This clinic, founded by Dr. William J. Rea, is the premier MCS treatment center in the world. I was familiar with their protocols and regimens and had previously consulted them about sauna therapy. They routinely used oxygen for their patients. I received the ceramic mask right away, but had to wait months for the stainless steel tubing because it was hand-made by one person. In the meantime I used tygon tubing, repeatedly boiled to reduce the smell.

The oxygen helped me cope, but I continued to slide downward. Driving became a nightmare due to increased sensitivity to gasoline and traffic fumes. Stores became like chemical factories to me. I stopped driving. I stopped going out. I became more sensitive to everything and retreated to my bedroom more and more.

I could no longer use the washing machine to do my laundry. The residue from my family's clothes contaminated my clothes and made them non-wearable. I hired someone to come in and wash my stuff by hand in the bathtub with baking soda.

My liver was overloaded and couldn't process toxins anymore. I started having daily liver pain, especially after meals. It would have been a relief not to eat, but my body was famished and starved for nutrients. So I ate and immediately afterwards breathed pure oxygen to mitigate the distress.

Previously I had been able to normalize my sleep cycle by employing a specific technique to reset my circadian rhythms, even though my sleep quality had remained extremely unrefreshing, disturbed, and abnormal. Now, not only was my sleep cycle disrupted once again, my sleep quality was further degraded, leading to a cascade of more insomnia and broken sleep, more exhaustion and weakness, more neurological stress and disruption.

My legs began to constantly hurt and burn, as if they were made of lead, and felt like they were literally on fire. I would elevate them 90 degrees against the wall to try to get some relief, and ice them down with ice packs. But it was no use. Nothing relieved this pain, it was relentless and punishing.

The old inflammation and burning in my chest and torso returned. The systemic viruses in my nervous system reactivated. My irritable bladder escalated to become a stinging, burning bladder. My brain was in continual reaction, pulsating with feverish heat and inflammation. In an attempt to cool off I would secure ice packs directly onto my head. My intolerance to noise worsened, and for the first time I became sensitive to light. I couldn't think, couldn't concentrate, all my senses and nerves strained, jumbled and on edge. I was crashing under the pressure of overstimulation and hyperreactivity to everything. I was experiencing a total meltdown, with my entire organism disrupted, impaired, muddled, enervated, swamped, devastated, overwhelmed, and tortured.

I fell deeper and deeper into a void of suffering and misery, a chasm of dejection. I felt anxious, depressed, and hopeless. I cried every single day for months. I was in despair. Twice a week I spoke to my psychotherapist on the phone while lying in bed, and sobbed through the entire session. She was great, remaining present and supportive of me through my anguish and torment, but she could change nothing for me.

While this was happening to me, life went on around me as usual. I couldn't understand this. Why wasn't anybody noticing that my body was self-destructing, that I was in danger, that I needed help, that I was losing the integrity of my mind? I felt like I was trapped underwater, drowning, struggling, and no one on land could see me or hear me.

It took me years to understand that when you are seriously chronically ill, people stop listening to you after a while. They expect the same song and dance from you, so they tune you out. When things worsen and you try to explain this, they don't get it: they can't imagine how your symptoms could be worse, because they truly don't understand your unusual symptoms in the first place. Or they don't want to get it: they just think you're complaining louder than usual.

I was in severe crisis, trapped, with no way out. I had run out of everything: doctors, treatments, and environmental safety zones; adjustments to my lifestyle, restrictions, and accommodations for my conditions; the goodwill and understanding of the people around me. And all my personal inner resources were evaporating and disintegrating. The world was continuing on its merry way, but my world was ending.

Desperate to end my relentless torture, I contacted the Hemlock Society to find out what options were available for someone in my impossible situation. I immediately found out that physician-assisted suicide and euthanasia are illegal. If I wanted to commit suicide, I was on my own. Not being a violent person,

I had no clue how to possibly go about it. I had just spent the last 10 years figuring out how to live within my ever-shrinking limitations, and now I had to shift gears and learn how to die. Each method I pondered had drawbacks, in addition to the possibility of failure. The easiest and most accessible for sick and debilitated people is an overdose of drugs with a plastic bag over the head. In the future, I would know two seriously ill individuals, one of them a friend, who took their lives this way. My objection to this method was due partly to its irony: the last thing I wanted was more chemicals to deliver me from the catastrophe that chemicals had wrought. It was distasteful and abhorrent.

No, I wasn't prepared to take my own life, but I was desperate for my suffering to end. I wanted assistance, support, compassion, understanding, real caring about my suffering. I wanted someone to help me end my suffering, one way or another. But just as our society didn't have medical solutions to handle my harrowing illness and give me back life, so it didn't have compassionate choices to provide me with a dignified and humane way to die. This state of suspended animation is a deeply painful one faced by many severely ill and disabled individuals. We're not of this world any longer, but neither are we of the world beyond. We are exiles, forgotten, abandoned to our private hell.

14

Escape
1999

I now understood that nobody was going to rescue me, that all options were gone. The thing I feared most was losing my mind. The continual hyperreactivities, the constant agony of my symptoms, and the inability to escape my hell would eventually break down my neurological integrity, a final indignity from which I knew there was no return. I could not let this happen. Since mine was an enormous problem, I reasoned it required an enormous solution, so I started praying and asking for such a solution.

If only I could get a substantial settlement from the class action suit, I could hire someone to help me escape my situation, take me to Arizona, find me a safe house, assist me in various ways. For a while now, during my meditations and spiritual work, a particular dollar amount had been spontaneously and repeatedly popping into my mind. If this did indeed turn out to be the actual amount I would receive, it would not be sufficient to put this plan into action. I thought of other ways I could raise money, and contacted various foundations, but that turned out to be a dead end because, as I learned, organizations generally donate funds to groups and projects, but not to individuals.

An MCS friend heard my anguished cry for help and suggested I go to the Environmental Health Center in Dallas, EHC-D. Why would I do that? I had already tried several of their treatments on my own with little or no benefit. The sauna detoxification therapy had been ineffective for me. The oxygen therapy was a lifeline, but it certainly wasn't pulling me out of my crisis. The IVs were very helpful in the beginning, but in the end they created reactivity in my veins. Their preservative-free allergy shots were a vast improvement over the preservative-laden ones I had tried in the past, but at the stage I was in, allergy shots would be useless. The only treatment I hadn't had access to was one called ALF, made from a patient's own blood. The blood was extracted, cultured and potentiated in the lab, and injected back into the patient. It was supposed to bolster the immune system, probably not the best choice for my autoimmune condition anyway. So, no, the EHC-D was not the solution I was waiting for.

The one thing that was very attractive to me about the clinic was the fact that it was a clean, safe place. It had been created with safer building materials, including porcelain walls that required no painting. The air was constantly filtered, and no chemicals or fragrances were allowed on the premises. This sounded like heaven to me. Unfortunately I knew they wouldn't allow me to move in and live on site!

The second time I spoke with my MCS friend, she reiterated her suggestion that I go to EHC-D. Didn't she understand that I was too sick to go anywhere? I never even left the house anymore, how could I travel to Dallas? Even if I wanted to go there, it was impossible. Her repeated suggestion was sheer folly, although I recognized it as a well-intentioned attempt to give an offering, a somewhat misguided glimmer of hope to a desperate friend. Once again no, this was not what I needed. What I needed was safety from chemical onslaught, escape to a better place. Finding such a place. Finding help to get me to this place. Yet none of these things were on the horizon. But the message about EHC-D kept coming at me. Perhaps I should listen to it. Perhaps my impossible, preposterous predicament required the entertaining of an equally impossible, absurd idea.

A practical person wouldn't have done what I did, but I was fueled by an inner guidance which can sometimes look and sound illogical, but in reality is taking you outside of yourself to a wider plane of possibilities. Without any money, without the necessary mobility, without a way to travel, without any help, I started to act as though going to the EHC-D was a viable option.

The clinic had a Patient Educator who would talk to you on the phone and answer any questions you had. By acting like I was a prospective patient I took full advantage of this service, calling several times a week over the next few months, learning all the details of their operation, figuring out what, if anything, might be available or workable for me, trying to convince myself that this was the place to go to save my life.

I knew that many years before they had a hospital unit where extremely reactive patients were quarantined or isolated in a super clean environment, until their systems calmed down. That unit was long gone. What did they offer today? I learned that they had safe apartments for their patients to stay in during treatment. However, these were not available for long-term or permanent residency, and they were smack in the middle of the city. Further probing revealed the existence of an MCS-safe village or compound at the outskirts of Dallas where the sickest and most sensitive patients went, the ones who could not survive in the heavy pollution of a city, who needed fresh country air. Now this caught my attention. A glint of distant hope appeared within my field of vision.

Almost simultaneous to the strange restructuring that was happening in my mind, and to what I thought were surreal actions on my part, a new global settlement was being finalized in the silicone breast implant class action suit. When it was unveiled, it turned out to be very similar in terms and structure to the previous one that had collapsed. A total of 4.2 billion dollars would be paid out by several implant manufacturers to cover claims plus the expenses of the multi-district litigation. The payments would be made without admission of culpability or acknowledgement of the link between silicone and disease. The women's compensation ranged from $5000 to $250,000. This meant that the average amount received would be only $26,000, one third of

which would go to the woman's attorney. It was not
a day for rejoicing. It was a day for closing this legal
chapter of the silicone breast implant saga.

The medical chapter would not and could not be
closed. In 2006 the FDA decided to lift the ban against
the manufacture, sale, and marketing of silicone gel
breast implants. There's now a new generation of women
with silicone gel coursing through their bodies, setting
up the terrain for more injuries and illnesses. I think of
this as round two of the unofficial experiment. The fact
that closed capsulotomies are no longer recommended
as a remedy for capsular contracture will prevent many
ruptures, but not all, and is no protection against the
biochemical effect of silicone upon the human organism.
I wonder how many rounds it will take to acknowledge
the truth and stop poisoning women's bodies.

The level of compensation I was eligible for turned
out to be the exact amount I had been intuiting all
along. The suspense was finally over. Now I knew that
what would remain of this amount, after paying my
lawyer's fee would not finance my grand Arizona dream.
Instead, I would have to spend it very carefully and
wisely, so it could last the rest of my life. After receiving
the net payment my conversations with the EHC-D
stopped being merely theoretical, and took on a tone of
reality and feasibility. Now at least I had the financial
ability to go to the MCS village if I wanted to, but all
the other elements were still missing.

The Patient Educator told me that no one would
hold my hand in Dallas. If I was extremely ill, I needed

to have a caretaker with me. Well, I didn't have a caretaker, nor did I have anyone available to take on such a role. The woman who ran the MCS village told me that at one time they had a van transporting patients to the clinic every day, but no longer. However, there was usually an MCS driver with a safe car who could be hired privately. This would solve the problem of going to appointments, doing errands, and so on. They also had a woman, a former patient, who did cooking for hire for those who needed it. This could be a tremendous help. So now we had a safe place to live, a driver, and a cook. This was starting to sound more plausible. Maybe I didn't need a caretaker after all.

As I continued to learn more about the situation in Dallas, I realized that the EHC-D had created a de facto community around itself, which was exactly what I was looking for. Having lost my membership in the normal, healthy world, and feeling like an exile who didn't belong anywhere, I craved my own specialized group to belong to. The fact that I had so many diagnoses and conditions made it even more difficult for me. Once my MCS became severe, I lost touch with most of my CFS and FM friends because they could continue to inhabit the real world. I also lost touch with many silicone-injured women because they got better, were not chemically sensitive or only slightly so, or were too sick to keep up friendships. It seemed that the only people who could have an understanding of what I was going through, were other MCS people who were sick enough to go to Dallas.

The biggest obstacle I faced was getting there. I could not survive a 1500 mile car trip. I also could not fly because commercial planes are enclosed environments layered with carpeting and upholstery containing formaldehyde. They are sprayed routinely with pesticides, use recycled air, and carry hundreds of normal people wearing perhaps hundreds of fragrances and chemicals. What other alternatives were there? I thought of air ambulances which carry critically ill patients to specialized hospitals. Would I qualify for this? In my mind I certainly did, in fact I felt this was exactly the intervention I needed. But I knew bureaucracy wouldn't agree. But who arranges for air ambulances, and how, and under what conditions? I decided to find out. In the Yellow Pages I found several listings for air ambulance companies. What I learned is that anyone can hire an air ambulance for transport, and that to go from Newark, NJ to Dallas, TX would cost $10,000. The planes are usually Lear jets stripped down to approximate the antiseptic conditions of an operating room, carrying oxygen and other life-saving equipment, staffed by a nurse, a paramedic and two pilots.

When I explained my extreme and unusual medical needs, there was no hesitation whatsoever: all the companies I spoke with were more than willing to follow my exact guidelines to ensure the safety of the plane's environment and staff, including using designated products to wash down the plane's interior surfaces and launder the staff's uniforms. Upon inquiring if there was any way to bring the cost down, I was told that if mine was not an emergency, and I could wait for a return flight, it would only be $6,000.

All of this positive information appeared to be shaping up as the big solution I had asked for. I started feeling happy that I could save my life, that I had found a place and situation to go to, as well as a way to get there. I couldn't believe how many barriers I had overcome.

There was one more thing holding me back: I was really scared to go alone. What if once I got to Dallas I was simply too sick to take care of myself, and do what was necessary? What if the set-up there wasn't sufficiently supportive of my needs? I would be stranded, alone. Since I could bring two additional people on the air ambulance, I invited two MCS friends to go with me. They wouldn't be caretakers, but they could provide emotional support and strength in numbers. If anything went wrong in Dallas, we could collectively get ourselves out of it. Unfortunately neither person was in a position to take the trip at the time. So I was on my own. I struggled with this for many, many weeks, feeling terrified, shaky, unsure, and extremely vulnerable. Finally I realized I just had to vanquish my fears.

My big solution had been presented to me, piece by piece, and now I was being asked to put aside my doubts, take a leap of faith, and go with it, all by myself. This was my path, my journey. I needed to call forth my courage and follow my fate.

It was the very beginning of July 1999 when I made my decision to leave. It was a major decision because I knew it was a one-way trip. There was no coming back.

I was leaving behind my old life with all its attachments and connections, and going towards something new and unknown.

The allowance on the air ambulance was one suitcase and one carry-on bag. I would have to say goodbye to my beloved crystals, books, goddess room and many other meaningful possessions. I made my preparations and waited for a return flight to be available in the Newark area.

As I waited I became more confident that this was the right thing to do. That no matter how things turned out, I needed to do this to save myself. I freed myself from all internal vacillations, impediments and judgments, and saw myself as going on an adventure. I became excited and impatient to leave.

On July 29th a nurse and a paramedic arrived at the house by limousine to pick me up. As I said my goodbyes to my family, my father started crying, wanting to keep hugging me and not let me go. He was the only one who understood I wasn't coming back. He knew he would never see me again.

PART II

TEXAS

15

Success

My entire experience with the air ambulance service was phenomenal. I don't think I've ever been treated so well, anywhere. All my guidelines and requests were followed to the letter, including that the limousine be smoke- and fragrance-free. We left from a small airport, where I was not subjected to crowds. The only thing I smelled there, during the few minutes I waited before boarding, was jet fuel which was very strong and I didn't like at all. But once inside the plane I felt safe and comfortable. The interior was clean and odorless, with mostly metal surfaces. I brought sheets with me to cover my seat and the built-in bed, where I lay down for part of the trip.

The most unexpected detail was that the nurse and the paramedic were both male. All I can say is that my trip was even more enjoyable for that reason. To get the solicitous and full attention of two men who are trained to be caring is a woman's dream come true! These two guys took great care of me, making sure I felt OK at all times, frequently asking me want I needed, allowing me to rest when I wanted to, and talking to me and helping to relieve my anxiety at other times. I even received a head and neck massage when I developed a headache from the loud noise the aircraft made.

It was a long trip and I was very fatigued of course, but the environment was chemically safe and all my reactions calmed down. My body was able to let go to a large degree, in spite of the fact that I was in a novel and therefore stressful and excitable situation. The inflammation and burning sensations eased off, and I was able to finally take a breath and feel some relief. After so many dreadful months of sheer and unending torture, this was a turning point.

In Dallas we landed at Love Field, the same airport where President John F. Kennedy arrived on the day of his assassination. That historic day, November 22, 1963, was the last day of his life. But this day, July 29, 1999, was the first day of my new life.

I wished I could have taken my nurse and paramedic with me and kept them as my very own personal attendants. But my allotment of fulfilled dreams was limited to one. I didn't need their assistance in getting to the MCS compound, so it was time to let them go, thank them for their wonderful work, and say goodbye. I got into the limousine and started on the last leg of my trip. My destination was a small town called Seagoville, about a half hour southeast of Dallas.

It was late afternoon, 106 degrees, sunny and very dry. As we got on the highway I noticed how spacious everything is in Texas. Right away I liked it. As we traveled away from the city and passed suburb after suburb, the areas became progressively less congested. I began to feel peaceful. By the time we pulled up at Ecology Housing, we were in a rural area. I was thoroughly exhausted, but calm and happy. I had arrived at a fabled place. All was quiet, natural, simple, and green. The compound, which everyone called the camp, is situated on several dozen acres of land so is isolated from traffic, main roads, and neighbors. I stepped out of the limousine and felt awash in serenity, tranquility, and stillness. My hell was over.

The Seagoville camp consists of various porcelain and aluminum trailers, and other buildings with porcelain-covered walls. Each unit is sparsely furnished and includes a bed, an air conditioner, and a TV enclosed in a TV box built into a wall, so the fumes vent to the outside. There is a large building called the cook shack where all the tenants prepare their meals at three stoves, and each is assigned a refrigerator. In another section of it there are a dozen washers and driers. I was shown into a small trailer and collapsed into bed.

I woke up to another dry, sunny, 106 degree day. I loved it. I familiarized myself with the camp, met some of the other residents, and arranged for a driver. Delivery of organic food and bottled water was available on a weekly basis, but I needed some supplies to tide me over until the next delivery day. I also wanted to go to the Environmental Health Center to check it out and schedule a consultation with Dr. William Rea. Even though I didn't expect much help, now that I was in Dallas and had the financial means, I owed it to myself to consult the preeminent MCS expert.

That first week was very hectic as I worked to organize myself, settle in, and get used to everything. Most of the other tenants left for the clinic each morning and returned in late afternoon or early evening. That grueling schedule was not for me. I was having enough trouble dealing with the camp. The constant walking between my trailer and the cook shack was too much for me, especially in the heat. It was 106 degrees every single day. And it became apparent that the air conditioner was simply not effective in cooling down a metal trailer bombarded by very hot solar rays. My body went into extreme inflammation and heat prostration. I couldn't stay there.

The only alternative was the EHC-D condominiums in the city. I knew I wouldn't do well in the city, but I had no choice. I needed to cool down my body and be in a smaller space to minimize my physical movements. I was driven into Dallas and moved into a condo which I found very safe and comfortable: ceramic tile floors, metal and glass furniture, old paint, cotton linens, water filters, and a very powerful and blessed air conditioner. Within a few days my inflammation and heat symptoms subsided, but soon thereafter my brain got weaker and weaker and then seemed to stop working. I felt like I did that time driving through Manhattan, only this time there was no tunnel to traverse to safety. For days I lay in bed unable to get up, debilitated, weak, sick, confused, unable to make decisions.

Needless to say at this point I felt completely defeated. The thing I had feared the most had happened. My Dallas escape had failed. Contemplating a return trip home was torment. It was a death sentence. I couldn't go back.

I begged a friend of mine to come to Dallas to help me, because I wasn't functioning. As much as he wanted to, being sick and chemically sensitive himself, he just couldn't. What he did instead was step in with his clarity of mind to substitute for the one that had gone missing in me. He suggested I call around and ask about any other possible sources of safe housing. After two frustrating and discouraging days of not being able to reach anyone and get any information, I finally tracked down a driver who told me of two private homes outside of Dallas that rented rooms, and took me to look at them.

The first was in a suburb 20 minutes away, and as soon as I walked in I smelled mold and mildew, so I walked right out. The second was only a few minutes from the Seagoville camp, in that same rural, peaceful area. It was a pretty house, well maintained, a brick ranch on a cement slab, with plants and flowers in front, and several birdfeeders, ceramic tile floors throughout, each room furnished with either metal and glass or old wood, central air conditioning, a large cooking area set up for the renters in an adjoining garage so that cooking odors would not infiltrate the house, and a spacious and beautiful back yard.

The house belonged to the woman who did cooking for some of the patients at the camp. She had actually cooked for me the first week, but for some reason had not told me about her house. Perhaps she didn't have a vacancy at the time, or didn't want to appear to be "stealing" patients from the camp or clinic. I toured the house with her and then was left alone to sniff and smell and determine how I felt in the environment. I already felt better away from the city, and I loved the house. I told her I would move in the next day.

The following afternoon I arrived and took up residence in the front bedroom, a cheery and sunny midsize room with a walk-in closet. Its walls were covered with heavy duty aluminum foil to seal in any lingering emanations, after being scrubbed and scoured numerous times to obliterate the fragrances from the previous owner. Aside from this one "anomaly" it was charming and well-appointed with delicate cotton curtains and bedding, and elegant glass shelving and night stands. I was very satisfied.

That night I went out in the backyard and reclined in a chaise lounge under the canopy of the wide Texas sky. Millions of stars quivered above me. A pleasant, still night air surrounded me. As I reflected on what had transpired, gratefulness sang and danced in every one of my cells, and poured out of me in waves. By being led to this place, with the right combination of features, I was finally reconnected to the tenuous and precious thread of life. I had succeeded.

16

Community

Most people with MCS are only lightly or moderately affected. They are not debilitated and don't have additional conditions such as CFS or FM. They can travel, camp out, and search for safer places to live. Some can design, plan and supervise the building of their own chemical-free houses. Others purchase regular houses and remediate them to make them livable. This is what Shirley did, the woman whose house I now resided in. She had previously lived at the camp for several years, undergone Dr. Rea's treatment program and recovered quite a bit of her health. She had put a lot of work into her house, and I was the beneficiary.

Living in that house allowed my body to rest and calm down. Each afternoon I could be found meditating and relaxing under the big juniper tree in the backyard. This was my private spot. It was wonderfully rejuvenating to spend those hours outdoors every day. Also, the cooking area was kept open to the outside at all times, and since this is where everyone congregated, I ended up spending most of my day in fresh air. What a boon to my overloaded and toxic body!

The house was a very social place with lots of comings and goings. Two of us were long-term tenants, but the third bedroom saw a constant turnover of guests who were there for short-term visits to the clinic. A friend of Shirley's was there on most days to help out. A cleaning woman came several times a week. And a neighbor dropped by frequently. Every Friday night our food was delivered from one of the Whole Foods stores in the city by a service called Store-to-Door. The person who started this service was a very friendly and enterprising young man we got to know because we were his last stop of the day, and he would sit down and visit with us. For a period of time a chiropractor came to the house each week to treat all of us. During another period we had a church group visit us weekly to support and minister to us. MCS friends from the Seagoville camp and other parts of Dallas would often visit and hang out. And on several occasions we hosted holiday parties and get-togethers for dozens of MCS people.

It was a balm to my soul to be in this kind of community atmosphere where everyone was in the same boat, no explanations were needed, and the common language of MCS was spoken. Even more, it was great to be surrounded by healthy people who understood, accommodated and supported our special needs, rather than fought or disbelieved us. I had finally found the community I was looking for.

Now that I had achieved relief from torture and misery, I decided to go through parts of Dr. Rea's program just to give myself another shot at detox. Instead of following the intense schedule most patients did, I went at my own, much slower pace. With Shirley cooking for me, and Lawrence driving me, I felt able enough to spend each morning at the clinic over the next two and a half months. I started with sauna, which I kept up for a total of eight weeks, then added a more concentrated form of oxygen therapy for two weeks, ALF shots, and finally some allergy testing. None of this made any difference to my condition, which only reinforced what I already knew about it.

However, I enjoyed my time at the clinic, meeting many chemically sensitive people from all over the country, and other countries as well. Most of these E.I.'s—this is what we call ourselves, for Environmental Illness—would stay for a few weeks, then go back to their homes, having made improvements in many cases, armed with new knowledge on how to clean up their environments and live chemical-free lives. Three or four of the patients were women with silicone breast implant poisoning, all of whom responded much better to treatment than I did. They were all married and eventually returned to their families. But for me, the value of being in such a place lay in the safety of the environment, and the proximity to others like me, nothing more.

By November I stopped going to the clinic every day, and settled into my life at Shirley's house. I took over my own cooking and established a new routine. Of course my chronic symptoms continued to be a daily challenge, and some days were worse than others. But on the whole, I reveled in the wonderful Texas weather, which was unusually dry that year, and enjoyed the camaraderie of my fellow E.I.'s.

At times my housemate Julia and I would borrow Shirley's car and go to the local 7-11 to buy cookies. Neither one of us was strong enough to drive much, so whenever we went on these small excursions, we laughed about our big adventure out in the world. Other times an E.I. friend from the camp would pick us up and take us to the park, where all three of us would lie on the grass and laugh at our situation. Some of us were interested in astrology and numerology so for fun we gave each other readings. On a few occasions we gathered together for equinox and full moon healing circles under the night sky. At Christmas we were all invited to a big party in Denton, a suburb 45 minutes away, at the house of an E.I. couple. A bunch of us carpooled there in two cars and had a fantastic time.

Whether they were helped by Dr. Rea's treatments or not, the E.I.'s who were on extended stays at the camp and at the house, and with whom I had ongoing contact, were all focused on healing. So there was a constant exchange of information and discussions about other treatments, modalities, doctors and practitioners. Besides the extensive professional resources available through the EHC-D, Dallas boasts a large holistic and metaphysical community offering every therapy imaginable. Everyone was doing or trying all kinds of regimens and treatments, including psychotherapy and spiritual work. It seemed everyone was working on healing not only their bodies, but their entire lives. I liked being in this atmosphere because I had the same goal. We were all trying to recreate ourselves post-illness.

I renewed my spiritual, emotional, psychological and energy work with various therapists and practitioners, some of whom came to the house and worked with me outdoors. I augmented this with meditation sessions with some of my fellow E.I.'s and lots of conversations about our respective processes and insights. I now concentrated on bringing in a partner to fulfill the other part of my dream. Dallas is the best place to meet an E.I. man, and we had a few coming through the house. In fact sometimes there was quite a bit of drama among all the singles. I was definitely in the right place and had several opportunities to partner up. The first one actually came from an E.I. friend in New Mexico whom I hadn't met, but knew through letters and phone calls, and with whom I had a strong spiritual connection. When he proposed sharing an E.I. house in Santa Fe, I said yes. Later, after I learned more about New Mexico and about him, I realized it wouldn't work. My heart was set on Arizona and was looking for a deeper inducement in the romance department. Some time later one of my camp friends proposed the same exact thing, thinking that Taos, New Mexico, would be a good environment for both of us, where we could help each other heal. I knew this wouldn't work either, so I turned him down.

There were two other men I was interested in. One was not an E.I., but was part of our E.I. world. He liked me but didn't think he could deal with my limitations. The other was so similar to me in spiritual terms, I thought he was my soul mate. Unfortunately, as I got to know him, I realized he was rather immature and needed a lot more development. I wanted someone mature, an equal partner with whom to share all aspects of the E.I. life, good and bad. Knowing I couldn't stay at Shirley's house forever, I kept waiting and hoping for the right person to show up. Meantime there was a wedding at the camp between two long-term residents, a very hopeful and encouraging event for all of us.

Along with fellowship and romance, there was also conflict among us. No two E.I.'s have the same sensitivities and reactions and this can cause difficulties when living in close quarters. Some E.I.'s are better than others at dealing with this. We were all brought together because of E.I., but did not necessarily have much else in common. Very often I needed to distance myself from the intensity of this E.I. world and tend to my own world of rheumatic disease/CFS/FM, which E.I.'s didn't seem to understand. One time I had a tumultuous altercation with Julia over the use of the central air conditioning system. I was experiencing a high rate of inflammation in my tissues and needed to cool down. She refused to let me use the A/C because she was having a reaction to it. Instead of understanding my problem and working out a solution or schedule with me, she fought me day after day and caused me to deteriorate and get very sick. The fact that I had accommodated her special needs for months on end, apparently did not entitle me to the same consideration. Finally I appealed to Shirley, who ordered her to leave the house whenever I needed the A/C.

In the spring of 2000 I decided to get a computer. My driver, Lawrence, who was also an E.I., took me to a used computer store and I picked out a refurbished laptop which I thought might be outgassed enough for me. It was my first personal computer and I was excited about it. There was a Public Library down the street from the house, where I had gone a few times to use computers, but it was very toxic and I couldn't be in there long enough to get anything done. I was hoping my own safe computer would help me keep connected with the outside world.

The laptop turned out to have a mild fragrance, but that wasn't the worst of it. I limited my time on it in front of an open window each day, and put it out to outgas the rest of the time. After several days I noticed that I was feeling hyper and nervous, and the muscles and nerves along my spine were contracting in a very painful manner. I knew what this was, because several of my E.I. friends had this condition: it is called electromagnetic hypersensitivity or EHS. When Julia wouldn't let me use the A/C, it was because of her EHS reaction to it. To accommodate her EHS problem, there was no TV watching at the house. EHS is a growing problem in our highly electrified world of computers, cell phones, digital TV, smart grids, cell towers, and wireless technology. Many people with MCS develop EHS, and now it had happened to me.

I had 30 days to return the laptop, so I experimented with it by waiting several days until my symptoms calmed down, then I tried using it again. I also tried sitting further away from it. And I tried limiting my time on it even further. But it was no use. My symptoms always recurred, and actually intensified each successive time. I returned the laptop and got my money back, but the loss was a heavy blow. I had already known that talking on the telephone for long periods of time made me extremely tired and irritable, but I had always thought this was a function of the chronic fatigue syndrome. Interestingly, I had no problem with the A/C, probably because I made very little use of it, spending most of my time outdoors. To learn that my intolerances had now spread to electronics was an ugly and unwelcome surprise. Even though I knew that my condition was progressive, I never could have imagined such an outcome. On the other hand, now I had even more in common with some of my E.I. friends, and was in the right place to practice avoidance of electricity.

17

The Camp

During the summer of 2000 many E.I.'s left Dallas and scattered to various places. Things got very quiet until I was the only one left at the house. In September Shirley and I had a disagreement we couldn't resolve, and she asked me to leave. I was not surprised. I knew she preferred renters to stay only for short periods, as this cuts down on the potential for clashes and conflicts. I had been there over a year and during that time we had had our differences. It was time for me to go. I had hoped to leave with better prospects, but the only option was the camp, so I made arrangements to go there. Luckily it was almost autumn, so I wouldn't have the heat problem I encountered the year before. And this time, instead of a metal trailer, I moved into a spacious room in one of the stucco buildings.

Everything was quiet at the camp also. At full capacity it holds about 20 people, now there were less. One of my friends, Louise, was still there, who welcomed me and helped me get situated. And so was a guy I had met the previous year, Arnold, who had gone back home, gotten sick again, and come back. The other tenants were a new woman from California who had been injured by agricultural pesticides, the newly-married couple, two long-term residents who were so hypersensitive they hardly ever came out of their units, and the couple who owned and ran the place.

In contrast to Shirley's house, which was full of life, this place now seemed flat and disconnected to me. This was because most of the people I knew were gone, and those that were left tended to keep to themselves more. Even with a communal kitchen, living in individual rooms or trailers is not quite the same as living in a house—it is not as intimate, and people are not as compelled to get along or be friendly. And truly, the camp is mostly a place for people to crash and isolate from the world, while they work to recover their health. Socializing is not the priority.

The property the camp is located on used to be a gravel mining area. Today it consists mostly of lakes and ponds, trees and wild vegetation roughly surrounding the compound itself. When I moved in I started having allergic reactions to everything growing in and out of the water. But within a few weeks of the season changing, my allergies cleared. When it first came into existence in the early 1990s, Ecology Housing was set up strictly for MCS, as the current problem of EHS was unknown at the time. As a result everything there is electric, as opposed to gas-powered, which causes reactions in E.I.'s. There is a big electrical transformer right next to the building I was living in, with the breaker box for the whole camp right in front of my door. I quickly realized this was not a good situation for me. What's more, living inside porcelain-covered steel walls means that electricity continually bounces around the room, repeatedly blasting your body. I tried moving to the other side of the compound, but none of the available units worked for me, for one reason or another. It seemed that all the best units were already taken.

However, even on the side furthest away from the transformer, I felt the same uneasy pulsation in my body. In fact, everywhere I walked on the premises, I could feel electrical currents in the ground. Years later I learned that this is due to an improper grounding technique that was used at each structure, causing elevated magnetic fields as well as magnetic and electrical spikes, all of which I could feel adversely affecting my nervous system. One place I felt at peace was on the bluff, away from all the buildings. I often went there by myself or with my friend Louise to meditate and ground on the earth. Lying on the ground or hugging a tree helps to release the excess electricity in the body, as does taking a bath or a shower.

My campmate Arnold was also electrically sensitive. He had developed both EHS and MCS working with computers. We had many conversations about these topics and, being an engineer, he was always coming up with ideas to try to resolve our respective problems. But I knew nothing would resolve for me until I was able to leave the camp and live in a house again. Several of us were interested in moving to Arizona and creating a community of individual safe houses. There was a lot of talk about this. But of course we lacked the health and resources for such an ambitious project.

Over the fall and winter I spent a lot of time in the cook shack with Louise, making the best of my situation. When our Mexican workman, Frankie, came in on his lunch break, I practiced my Spanish with him. Behind the building there is a wonderful verdant area with a pond filled with turtles and egrets, and that is where I ate all my meals, on the patio—this was another peaceful spot for me. There was no car that I could borrow, so I felt stuck in a way that I never did at Shirley's house. And I didn't want to send for my car until I was more permanently settled somewhere else. Lawrence took me out occasionally to medical appointments or to do errands. When Dr. Alfred Johnson, an associate of Dr. Rea, opened his own environmental clinic, I switched to him and became his patient. In addition to doing everything Dr. Rea does, he takes Medicare and also offers osteopathic adjustments, which I need for my troublesome back.

As I waited for a new opportunity to arise or someone interesting to show up, I continued to do my inner work. Louise was on the same path, so we constantly shared our processes with one another. This was a highlight for me. I appreciated her friendship tremendously, because it was difficult to get close to anyone else. In spite of this difficulty, however, we were still a community, a special group of outcasts, linked by our common intolerance to the rest of the world. And that year our community had several losses. First, the woman from California went home. Shortly afterwards the newly-married couple found and bought an E.I. house in a remote part of Arizona where there is a small E.I. community, and left us. These were good losses. But we had bad ones too. A woman from the Chicago area, who had been a camp resident years before, came back to Dallas and moved into Shirley's house after I left. She continued to spiral downward and killed herself. A clinic patient and camp resident we all knew from the previous year, who had gone back to Hong Kong, worsened in that environment and took her own life. And the 85-year-old owner of the camp died, leaving his wife to run the place by herself.

As spring started coming around, a few new people arrived. Most had spouses or family members with them. I kept hoping for single people to show up with whom I could team up. I didn't feel good at the camp. I was struggling against the high electromagnetic frequencies all the time, and this dragged me down, both physically and mentally. I also felt stuck and isolated and missed the more social and friendly environment at Shirley's house. I wanted new friends and potential partners with whom to create a different living arrangement somewhere. But it just wasn't happening. So I started making calls.

I knew I had to leave the camp before summer because I didn't tolerate the heat. Summer is the busy season when the camp is full, and I could just foresee the mayhem in the cook shack, which I simply didn't have the physical energy to deal with. I would have been happy to remain in Dallas, if I could only find a safe house. I spoke to two women who were renting rooms in their respective houses, but neither was chemically-safe enough for me. I even inquired about a vacant house in a neighborhood nearby that I thought

I could share with roommates, but that didn't work out either. There was nothing else. I then realized that it was time to once again stretch my wings and fly solo.

Arizona was my dream, so I just had to make it happen, one way or another. I contacted all the areas where I knew E.I.'s lived, to find out about the housing situation. Very quickly I got in touch with a woman named Bernice, who was looking for a roommate in Prescott. We talked several times about her house, the town, the available services, all the important details I needed to know to make a decision. As before, this would be a one-way trip with no going back, so I had to be sure.

I had always pictured myself living in a hot desert city like Phoenix or Tucson, or in the mystical red rocks and vortexes of Sedona. Instead what I was getting was a small western town in the high mountain desert, two hours away from a metropolitan area. As someone who has always lived in or near cities, and relied on the plethora of services and choices that surround and radiate from them, I had concerns. But I knew I would do well in the house, and was encouraged by the large number of E.I.'s in the area. It seemed I could get the help I needed. It was a wonderful opportunity to finally go to Arizona, a place I imagined to be both my E.I. and spiritual home.

The Store-to-Door delivery service still came on Friday nights, and I still visited with the owner every week. He was in the process of getting his pilot's license, so I asked him if he might be able to fly me to my new home. Because he was still a student, he could not, but he told me about an organization called Airlifeline, which provides free flights to those in medical and financial need. The pilots are volunteers who donate their time and the use of their own private planes and fuel. I had hit the jackpot. This was perfect for me.

As I made my preparations to leave, the camp filled up with new residents. Louise wrote me a beautiful, heartfelt friendship letter. Others gave me cards and wished me well. On the morning of May 20, 2001 at 8:00 a.m. I stepped out of my room, going toward Lawrence's car in the parking lot, and saw all the camp residents standing outside on the central lawn, even those who normally didn't get up until noon, waiting to say goodbye to me and send me off as a group. I was very touched by this and got teary-eyed. This entire community, this whole place, had saved my life. It was bittersweet to leave it. I would miss it.

Lawrence drove me to a small airfield very close by, where I met the first of the two pilots who would ferry me to Arizona, and boarded his small plane. He would take me as far as El Paso, where the second pilot would be waiting to take me the rest of the way. As we took off and I waved goodbye to Lawrence, it hit me that I would probably never come back here again, or see any of these people again, and my tears flowed freely. I asked the pilot if we could circle over the camp for a last look, and we did. Later on, in a letter, my campmate Arnold wrote me that he saw the plane fly by and sent up a last salute and farewell. When a long-term resident leaves the camp, it is considered quite a feat. No matter where that person is headed, she has basically left the equivalent of a refugee camp, or a leper colony, or a hostage prison, and she is rejoining the world. Those left behind wonder when their turn will come.

I had high hopes for the next phase of my journey. The two years I had spent in Dallas were precious to me. They had plucked me out of my abyss. They had given me a sense of belonging again. They had been a unique experience. I saw them as a bridge between my old life and my new life. I felt I was now going towards the fulfillment of my dream—the house, the partner, the community, the spiritual environment. I was finally on my way to Arizona!

PART III
ARIZONA

.

18

Prescott, Arizona
2001

In life nothing ever turns out the way you expect.

Once again I landed at Love Field, this one in Prescott, AZ. This should have been a good omen. But I was sick the whole way from El Paso, TX, throwing up in a paper bag, and this was a bad omen as I had never, ever before been sick on a plane.

The house was a rental, an old house that had never been renovated. With the landlord's permission and the help of her husband and son, Bernice cleaned it up and made the changes she needed, including removing the carpet, sanding the varnish off the kitchen cabinets, and sealing the inside of drawers with aluminum foil and aluminum tape. When I arrived, she had already lived there nine years. Her husband had recently passed away, and her son had married and moved out. I did well there, and was happy to be in a house again.

Now I concentrated on getting to know all the E.I.'s in town, and finding a driver and a shopper. Contrary to what I had been led to believe, this turned out to be very difficult. Whereas in Dallas there was quite a bit of organization and cohesion among the E.I.'s, this wasn't the case in Prescott. There seemed to be various categories, groups and cliques within the community that tended to keep themselves separate and do their own thing. There was no real community consciousness. I was dismayed by this. In Dallas most people were very interested in sharing and connecting with others, and feeling part of a unique group. But in Prescott practically no one seemed curious about me as the new person in town. And no attempts were made to return my friendliness or get to know me. Coming from the Dallas experience, that was strange and hurtful to me. I felt unwelcome and rejected. I was truly taken aback by this development, and just couldn't figure out the indifference among a group of marginalized people who, one would think, needed all the friends they could get, and would want to stick together with as many of their kind as possible. I'm still trying to figure this out.

Apparently in Prescott simply having MCS is not enough. You need to be a high-functioning E.I. to score friends. I suppose if I had been male, with a car or truck, and able to hike or do other similar activities, I would have been an instant hit. As it was, I could only be myself, and continue to hope to connect with someone at some point. I missed Dallas terribly, every day. Thank God for Louise, who called daily and cheered me up, and my pen-pals and other long-distance friends. Still, I had come to this place not to feel lonely, but to be in community, and I just wasn't feeling or finding it either in actuality or in spirit.

I was not able to find a shopper, so I asked the local health food store if they would shop for me and send the groceries by taxi, and they agreed. Getting good-quality water delivered was a problem. Other kinds of shopping were difficult, so I mostly did without. There was no regular driver to hire, but a few of the E.I.'s gave me rides now and again. I was on the phone every day trying to find services, deliveries, rides, people to help me, and personal connections. It was frustrating that it just wasn't shaping up the right way for me, and I thought about moving back to Dallas. Unfortunately, there was no place to go back to. But I continued to keep my ears and eyes open for any situation anywhere that might be better for me.

In the fall I decided to send for my car, which had sat in my parents' driveway for two years. I had apprehensions about driving and taking on my own errands again, but all I could do was try it. When the car arrived, I couldn't tolerate its smells. After removing the floor mats, I left it in the front yard with all the windows rolled down, to bake and outgas in the Arizona sun for many weeks, until I could finally get in it and not become sickened. Very gradually I eased myself into driving to various places around town. This took a very long time because I could only drive occasionally, when I felt up to it. It helped that the town is small, uncongested and unpolluted.

From an environmental perspective Prescott is a great town for E.I.'s. From most other perspectives, however, it was not a good fit for me, and I knew this early on. One of my counselors, however, told me that it takes time, years even, to adjust to a new place and create a life. So I kept up my positive expectations in the ensuing months and years, as I continued to reach out both inside and outside the E.I. world, and within my limitations tried to create meaning and purpose, support and networking. But it seemed virtually impossible to make friends and find people I had anything in common with. It was very surprising that none of the E.I.'s were metaphysically oriented, or had undergone a spiritual transformation like I had. Possibly this had to do with the fact that most of them had not been in the kind of dire circumstance I had been in, were not debilitated and hampered to the degree I was, and were not facing a progressive and worsening course in their condition. They had not descended into hell, and had not had the Seagoville camp experience of total separation from the outside world. The kindred spirits I was looking for were nowhere to be found.

I kept hoping some of my old friends would end up moving here, and that family and friends would visit me. I kept hoping to meet a companion, or that I would find a better situation. I was living strictly on hope.

By 2003 Bernice got remarried and moved out, and I had the house all to myself. This was both a blessing and a curse. Because the house was small, really a one-person house, it was good to not be cramped anymore, be able to spread out and make the space my own. But I felt unsupported for the responsibility. I wasn't well enough to handle the demands of an entire house by myself. The reason I had moved in with a roommate in the first place was to share both companionship and burdens, and now neither of those had panned out.

My dream just wasn't coming together. This was the wrong place for me. I longed to leave and go somewhere else. I yearned for the belonging I had had in Dallas. Although I had found a safe place to live, I had lost everything else that mattered to me.

In March of 2004 the house was put up for sale and I was given a 30-day notice to vacate it. I decided not to panic, knowing that things always work out the way they're supposed to. On the one hand I felt elated that this development might finally propel me out of Prescott and into a better place. On the other hand I feared becoming homeless if I could not find another place I tolerated. Many E.I.'s are indeed homeless, living out of their cars, or in tents in remote areas. Because of all my other physical problems, I could not survive in those situations.

The other option was to buy the house and remain safe. I felt extremely ambivalent about this because I knew that owning the house would mean being stuck here forever, with no possibility to fulfill the rest of my dream. It was a depressing thought, but I didn't have much time, so I had to act. I talked to family and friends about the circumstances, and my sister offered to buy the house and become my long-distance landlord, thus saving me from homelessness. In the end I didn't have a choice, as there weren't any safe places I could move to, so the deal was done. I was profoundly grateful to my sister, but at the same time felt trapped and dispirited. My dream had died.

19

Destiny

Why had I been guided to Arizona, my way there made so easy, only to find the opposite of what I had visualized? What was this about?

I felt very alone and untethered and had resentment and bitterness towards the E.I.'s for not being who I needed them to be. I also resented Prescott and all of Arizona for being such a resounding disappointment. This was definitely not my home. This was my prison.

When I read Aleksandr Solzhenitsyn's The Gulag Archipelago I found myself identifying with those Russians who were disappeared, tortured, and imprisoned in forced labor camps far from their homes, never to see their families and friends again. Here I was disabled, chronically ill, and basically housebound—what did this have to do with political prisoners in a totalitarian state? On the face of it, nothing at all. But at the psychological level, it was exactly the same: I felt like a prisoner, tortured by my symptoms every day, disappeared from the normal world, far away from family and friends, forced to labor to exhaustion each day to survive and take care of myself, with no one looking out for me day to day, weighed down by isolation and loneliness, pondering a long sentence with no end in sight, and nothing to look forward to except more of the same suffering.

Both experiences comprise massive losses, profound deprivations, and constant mourning.

My father died at the end of 2001 and as I couldn't go back for his funeral, I was left bereft to grieve alone. A close MCS pen pal of five years was no longer able to correspond with me when she developed cervical cancer and died three months later. My friend Louise got better and distanced herself both from me and other E.I.'s who were not improving. My only Prescott friend, a funny, intelligent MCS woman with whom I had great conversations, lasted only a few months in my life, as she had a stroke and died soon thereafter. Another friend with whom I had a long-standing and long-distance relationship became able to take classes and work part-time, and no longer had time to write or keep in regular touch with me.

These people constituted the fabric of my support system, and within a very short time they were all gone, leaving no replacements, just deep empty chasms.

Several years later I would lose even more relationships as, once again, a block of people exited my life en masse. These cluster losses leave you feeling ripped apart and torn asunder, like a chunk of you is gone forever. These were not deaths, however, but the sudden blowing up or petering out of friendships which caught me unawares, leaving me feeling deserted, abandoned and discarded. I was so distraught I read several books on the subject. Learning that these types of occurrences are common, and do not reflect upon my desirability as a friend, made me feel better. But I was still left reeling, shell-shocked at the sheer numbers, suddenness and speed of them, and the resulting utter emptiness and sorrow.

I've now been in Prescott for more than 10 years, and in all that time I've seen my mother only once for three days, when she came to visit with my sister/landlord. Another time my youngest sister and her husband visited, also for three days. That's it. The rest of my family, including three nephews and one niece I barely know, I haven't seen at all. Being separated from my family for such a long period of time, without physical, person-to-person contact is like not having a family at all. Sure, we keep in touch by phone, and send cards, but there are no more shared experiences and no building of new memories. Their lives have continued as before, unchanged in their trajectories, while my life took a detour to a distant place, a lonely gulag. They may miss me, but they still have each other, they are still together. But I don't have them anymore. I'm like an orphan.

My Prescott experience has been one of losing people and becoming more and more isolated, which is the most painful and difficult deprivation of all. In comparison, dealing with the loss of my health, career and previous life was a breeze. Even dealing with my severe physical symptoms and chemical and electrical exposures is much, much easier for me than facing the daily pain of isolation. All of the above have remedies, however inadequate and incomplete they may be. But isolation and seclusion have no remedy: they are at the outer limit of human experience. They can only be suffered and endured alone.

Through the years I've worked with various counselors and psychotherapists to keep myself going. This has always been via telephone, which Medicare doesn't pay for. But I've been fortunate to find caring individuals willing to accommodate me financially. Sometimes those wonderful professionals were the only ones giving me kind words and making me feel human. However, this makes for a pseudolife. It is no substitute for personal friends and intimates, and my loneliness and desolation never left.

As a metaphysician I've always tried to understand the forces behind the events in my life. Patterns have always been apparent to me. There is a recurrent theme that is very clear now. In 1968 when I immigrated to the U.S., I lost my whole world. In 1988 when I collapsed, the life I had fell away. In 1999 when I went to Texas, I left everything behind, to start over. And in 2001 when I came to Arizona, I moved on to what turned out to be the barest existence of them all. Each time I moved further west there was a further restriction, a downsizing, a scaling back. Each time I forfeited a world, and relinquished more of my life and my being, until I was stripped to the bone.

I've always acted to contravene this theme by focusing all my energy to build up a normal life, a life of gain not loss, an average life of contentment, accomplishment, and fulfilling relationships. This, of course, is what most people do and more or less succeed at. But for me it didn't work. Destiny cannot be fooled with. This is in spite of the persistent message we receive from our American culture that we can be anything we want to be, that we have the free will to choose and create what we want, which isn't quite true. Bruce Lipton, PhD, cellular biologist and internationally recognized authority in bridging science and spirituality, says that 95% of life is lived through the programming in our subconscious mind. This means that our free will is limited to 5%, not a lot to work with.

The way I see it, free will is the tool we use to accept, adjust to, and make the best of what we are given. What we are given is our fate, our destiny, which must be lived out. The reason our destiny must be lived out is that it has a purpose, higher than what is visible on the physical plane.

It was my destiny to end up in the desert of Arizona, and experience all the qualities that a desert exemplifies: barrenness, emptiness, desolation, solitude, isolation, desiccation, depletedness, deprivation. It took me a long time to accept this. I fought it for many years, still wanting to believe I had come here to fulfill my original vision, and trying over and over again to figure out a way to make it happen. In the end I had to accept what was.

But I still didn't know what was behind it. What was the purpose of such a destiny?

20

Purpose

Earlier in my illness I thought perhaps my purpose was that of the "wounded healer," the archetype of the injured individual who goes through a deep, personal transformation, learns how to heal himself, and then is able to help others heal. I envisioned becoming a counselor or holistic practitioner and helping others come through the same ordeal that I had. But although I did indeed undergo a spiritual transformation, I was not able to heal myself. So this wasn't my path.

The pressure to get well from chronic illness is tremendous, and it is everywhere, from self-help and spiritual books, to alternative practitioners who tell you they can heal you, to family and friends for whom your disability is an inconvenience, to well-meaning neighbors and strangers who offer useless advice, to fellow sufferers who have gotten well and want to foist their treatments upon you. I feel this pressure even to this day after 23 years of disability. I have often succumbed to it by trying one more supplement, one more treatment, one more doctor, always unsuccessfully. Just as often I've resisted it, sending out the message that I don't need to be fixed, I just need to be accepted.

Even worse than this pressure is the blame and judgment that is hurled at those of us who don't get well. We are told: you don't want to get well; you still haven't found the right treatment; you're not disciplined enough; you're not spiritual enough; you don't believe strongly enough that you can get well. I'm always amazed and appalled at this because the same blame and judgment would never be directed at someone confined to a wheelchair. It seems only invisible disabilities are fair game. Whether you recover from chemical injury depends on the following: the type of injury, the extent of the injury, the location(s) of the injury, and the duration of the injury. All the rest is irrelevant.

No, I'm not a wounded healer, I'm simply wounded. As such, I next came to believe that my purpose was to join forces with other wounded individuals, to create an ideal E.I. community of support and mutual assistance, an example to the rest of the world not only of how to create safety for the chemically injured, but also of the cohesion, unity, acceptance, non-judgment, inclusion and love that the wounded need. Chemical injury, and all other emerging, poorly understood, complex diseases need acceptance in our world. They need visibility, accommodation and compassion. A solid E.I. community would be an ambassador for the propagation of this message.

Unfortunately, the E.I. community is splintered and is no such ambassador. This is because personalities and egos get in the way, as do disparate levels of disability and symptom severity, as well as different and conflicting priorities and agendas. The E.I. world has not yet learned the lessons it needs to teach the rest of the world.

The dream of community had taken me to Arizona, but now it was clear that was not my purpose. I felt disenchanted, even deceived. Apparently we can be fooled, in the service of destiny. So what was my purpose? I was no longer receiving spiritual guidance and insights like before. I was at a loss. I couldn't believe I'd ended up this way, and no one seemed to understand or empathize with my situation. After a long time I grasped that my isolation was a special circumstance not shared by the majority of E.I.'s or even other chronically ill people, and that community was not important to them because they had no need for it.

Being present with myself and my experience was all I could do. Exploring the truth of my life was important, and I did this partly by reading the stories of others who, through dissimilar circumstances, also experienced isolation and all kinds of imprisonments and sufferings. I took refuge in those stories, and felt a kinship with those people. Another way to get to the truth was through consultations with psychotherapists, astrologers, spiritual channels and spiritual teachers. They all gave me bits and pieces of information that were useful, perceptive and valuable. With this input, I was able to validate and strengthen my own impressions, intuitions and feelings, and get clarity about my path. Finally, what became clear is that my purpose is karmic, connected to another lifetime.

It had never made any sense to me that we live, die, and then spend eternity in heaven or hell. This had always seemed like an arbitrary, simplistic story somebody made up. For one thing, it seemed to me heaven and hell are right here on earth. For another thing, humans are multilayered beings, vital and dynamic. Our nature is based on change, movement and growth. We are not static, we don't just go "hang out" forever somewhere. The complexity and multidimensionality of life make it unlikely that such a simple story can explain it. Part of this story is that we're sinners, condemned to go to hell forever unless we repent and change our ways. But I for one never felt like a sinner. On the contrary, because I was brought up to be a "good girl," I always felt pure, perfect, the upholder of the highest standards. I always did the right thing, always followed the rules, never had anything to confess or repent for. So where did that leave me? What was I doing here?

I am a very empathic person, which means I can feel and absorb other people's feelings, emotions and energies. It's like I'm permeable. I can also feel and absorb other vibrations and frequencies, like the movements of the planets and stars, which is why astrology is relevant for me. It's like I'm a receiving station, taking in information through osmosis. Intuitively, organically, cellularly I feel and sense certain things and I know them to be true. These things coincide with esoteric teachings and metaphysical writings. Many of these things are also being confirmed by modern-day science such as quantum physics and superstring theory. I am not a physicist, so I cannot explain things from that perspective. But I am a metaphysician.

Metaphysics means "beyond the physical." It is where science and spirituality intersect. According to this discipline, there are many levels of existence beyond our three-dimensional physical reality. There is the emotional level, also called the etheric level, which contains the blueprints for physical forms. There is the mental or reasoning level. And there is the higher mental level, where our collective unconscious resides, and is the realm of archetypes. The highest level is the spiritual one from where everything originates. Each level is an electromagnetic energy field which overlaps and interacts with the others. As humans we exist within all of these levels simultaneously. In addition, every one of our choices, acts, thoughts and feelings constitutes a vibration which goes forth like a wave, affecting everything and everyone in its path, eventually coming back around to us. This is basically what karma is.

The law of karma is constantly at work. It simply means that for every action there is a reaction or consequence. We also know it as the law of cause and effect and the law of balance. Positive karma increases our spirituality, while negative karma creates disharmony or misalignment in our spiritual energies. Both are interwoven in all of our lives. In the case of negative karma, we are given the opportunity to set things right and rebalance our spiritual essence. In the case of positive karma, we can choose to learn new lessons and continue to improve ourselves. Both are achieved by returning to earth reincarnated in new bodies, living new lives, and thus accomplishing new goals. This is an ongoing process requiring numerous lifetimes.

Billions of people around the world believe in reincarnation. We in the western world generally do not, because we're not familiar with it. This is because very early on in the history of the Catholic Church, all references to reincarnation were removed from the Bible. This was done so people wouldn't get distracted and would instead focus on following the church's teachings in the present lifetime. But reincarnation is actually the process we go through to prepare ourselves to ascend to a higher spiritual place.

Through it we have a wide variety of experiences on the physical plane, walk in the shoes of our fellow earthlings, and learn compassion. Reincarnation provides an explanation for the disparities in people's lives. It answers the question "Why do some humans have wonderful lives, and others miserable, painful ones?" Sooner or later, through reincarnation, we experience all kinds of lives, happy and unhappy, healthy and sick, mundane and tragic. In this manner we evolve and round out our beings, on our way to spiritual mastery.

I was aware of several past lives I had lived as a nun and a monk during which I purified myself and burned off a lot of negative karma. These accounted for the image I held of myself as a pure blameless person. I believed I had accumulated a lot of grace during those lives, and assumed I was done with any negative karma.

But my current experience wasn't reflecting that belief. My body was telling me otherwise, and my punishing isolation pointed to something else. Still, my self-image didn't permit me to entertain any information that didn't conform with it. So I was shattered when the last piece of the puzzle fell into place.

It came from a former counselor and spiritual teacher who is now my friend. He went into meditation and received this information about me from his spiritual guides: I chose my present lifetime in order to understand what I did in the 17th century, when I was a jailer of political prisoners who were tortured and kept in isolation in Europe. Words cannot express how humiliated, disgraced and ashamed I felt to have lived such a brutal, vicious life that caused such unspeakable pain and suffering to other human beings. I almost had a breakdown. Then my friend reminded me I am no longer that jailer, I have evolved, I am paying heavy dues for what I did, and am in the process of discharging that karma.

Ever since my spiritual awakening in the goddess room I had known I had a higher purpose. Finally I understood what that purpose was: to make amends for my actions by experiencing and comprehending at a deep cellular and psychic level the traumas and conditions I had inflicted on others, thus achieving a higher level of spiritual growth. This I could live with. This made sense to me. I was "taking my punishment" so to speak, for a very good cause: the deeper transformation of my spirit.

Understanding my past life karma and spiritual purpose has been crucial for me. It has been instrumental in allowing me to come to terms with and be at peace with my very private, still ongoing personal struggle.

21

Love Story

During my long, lonely years of disability the only thing I truly regretted in life was not falling in love. Missing out on the opportunity to fully and deeply love another human being in a devoted, intimate, profound way was more than I could endure. I did not want to die without it happening to me.

Even after getting breast implants I was never good at attracting men. This was always very frustrating for me. Eventually I learned that this is due to my life energy. My past lives as a nun and a monk are part of the archetypal life energy that I still carry and embody to this day. Another name for this archetype is V*esta,* the Greek temple goddess who was the keeper of the spiritual flame. As a contemplative, and unlike the other goddesses in the Pantheon, she did not have lovers, husbands or children. Her one friend was Hermes, also known as Mercury, the god of travel and communication who at times found refuge and rest in the temple with her. Personifying the *Vesta* prototype gives me a deeper, spiritual understanding of the world, and at the same time also keeps me from the average romantic entanglement. Ever hopeful, however, I'm always looking for the one true love of my life. Now I worried my time was running out, doomed never to experience what I consider to be the most sublime and fulfilling of human experiences.

Several months after arriving in Arizona I happened to communicate by telephone with a man named Robert, who lived in a different town quite a distance from me. We spoke once, and not again until many months later, at which point he decided to come to Prescott to visit me. Unlike the other Arizona E.I.'s, he wasn't interested in hiking or other physical activities, he just wanted good conversation and he got that with me. We were mentally compatible and had many things in common. Every few months he would come to Prescott and visit with me, and this is how we slowly got to know each other and became friends. Our communication was both calming and stimulating. We seemed to understand each other and have complementary personalities. The most important thing for me was how accepted I felt by him, and how appreciated as a person: he was interested in my background, my story, my experience and the knowledge I had accumulated as a result of it.

The problems with this friendship, however, were many. Because our interactions were infrequent, it wasn't possible to get close to him. He wasn't the type to stay in touch by phone, so except for the occasional call, the only times we talked were those when he came to visit. This wasn't enough for me. His availability was simply too limited for the kind of friendship I was looking for. This was due not only to the numerous health problems he had to attend to, but also to other personal and family matters which took up a lot of his time and energy. Of course I understood all this, but I was frustrated that having found someone I liked and felt comfortable with, who also liked and felt comfortable with me, I wasn't able to have the kind of relationship I needed and wanted. In point of fact, his friendship was at the periphery of my life, and did nothing to alleviate my daily loneliness and isolation.

I think the visits provided him with periodic relief and diversion from his own problems. But my problems were not being addressed, so I had to detach myself emotionally time and again. I really needed somebody close by, that I could count on, that had more time for me, that I could call on anytime. And it wasn't him.

In the fall of 2006 I went to see my rheumatologist who told me about a new drug that some of his MCS patients were taking and doing well with. He said he could give me free samples of it if I wanted to try it, and that I would know in seven days whether it worked for me or not. At that time my life felt empty and meaningless, so thinking I had nothing to lose, even with my history of adverse drug reactions, I decided to go ahead and try it. I took the Lyrica home with me and started it the next day.

Lyrica is an anti-seizure medication which has become the treatment of choice for fibromyalgia, and has thus singlehandedly put fibromyalgia on the social and cultural map through its TV advertising, allowing this once baffling condition to gain credibility and legitimacy. It works by acting on the hypersensitivity of the central nervous system which is assumed to be the cause of the muscular pain, and many sufferers get benefit from it. Going by that same principle, it is also prescribed for MCS, but not with the same results. I received no benefit whatsoever, and after several days started experiencing reactions. On day seven I took the last pill.

The following day I plunged into a suicidal depression. It was horrible. Knowing immediately that this was an effect of the concentration of Lyrica in my system was no help: I just wanted to die. All anti-seizure drugs have been linked to suicidal behavior, with some patients attempting or successfully committing suicide, some violently.

I wrote to Dr. Jack Kevorkian, who was in prison for helping a chronically ill person commit suicide. It was too late for him to help me, but I just wanted to communicate with him and let him know that I supported and admired him for the courage and compassion he displayed in helping those of us who no one else can help. I wondered if there were others out there who might help me and for this I needed the internet. Not knowing who to turn to for this, I decided to call Robert and ask him to do a search for me.

He and I had actually talked about suicide before, topping each other with the most creative way to do it, and laughing at the impossibility and absurdity of it: his was standing in front of a Japanese bullet train, mine was flying a plane into the side of a mountain. This kind of talk helps relieve the pressure and helplessness of unrelenting, chronic disease. You don't really want to kill yourself, but knowing that the option is there gives you a feeling of control over your uncontrollable life.

This time, understanding the state I was in, he knew I was serious. He didn't say much, but a few days later he came to see me. As soon as he walked in the door he told me he had something important to talk to me about. As we sat at my kitchen table, what came out of his mouth was something I never would have imagined in a million years. With tears in his eyes, he told me he was badly shaken by my wanting to seriously kill myself. He said he cared about me, and didn't want to lose me because I was his best friend! He would do whatever he had to in order to keep me alive, get me through my crisis, support me and be there for me! My crisis had shocked him, woken him up, and made him realize how much he needed me and wanted to be close to me!

I was stunned. Right in front of me he transformed himself. He opened his heart to me and I saw him with new eyes. It's like I was able to see inside him finally, to the place of his authentic self. He took my hands, drew me into an embrace, and held me. In that moment everything fell away, all invisible walls crumbled and pulverized, the world receded, and there was nothing but him and me.

That day our relationship changed completely. He rearranged his entire life to spend more time with me, driving into Prescott every week to see me, and talking on the phone between visits. All of his attention, caring and nurturing made me want to live, and helped me fight the suicidal depression. The struggle lasted about a month at the end of which my body finally cleared the after-effects of the Lyrica and my brain rebalanced itself. If it hadn't been for Robert, I don't know what would have happened to me. He was the only person who cared enough to recognize what I needed, and sprang into action. No one had ever rescued me before, and this man did, he saved my life. This man was my knight in shining armor, my hero.

Robert was the most amazing thing that ever happened to me in my entire life. He didn't simply save my life, he renewed and revitalized it. He reanimated my whole being, breathing new life into all the places that had shut down. He opened the floodgates to wonderful, lovely, shiny new gifts. He healed me.

For the first time ever I fell truly and deeply in love. This was the man I had waited and hoped for my whole life. This was my guy. Finally I had someone who belonged to me. I was no longer alone.

Our relationship was based on a foundation of friendship, so it was easy to build on that. Now it grew, blossomed and deepened. We related to each other and helped each other in all kinds of new ways, going beyond the mental interchange that had been the hallmark of our friendship, and expanding on the respect and admiration we held for each other. We became each other's best friend, support system, community and family. All the things I longed for I now had in one person. We were like a closed system, he and

I complete against the world. Even though there were many limitations, restrictions and challenges imposed by all our physical ailments, they did not affect the quality and depth of our affection. Our connection transcended physical impediments. A powerful energetic channel opened up between us, transforming our relationship into a deep spiritual experience.

I couldn't believe this had actually happened to me at the age of 49, after years of painful isolation and aloneness. It was the greatest gift I had ever received, truly a miracle. Being with Robert put solid ground back under my feet—I no longer felt lost, abandoned or left behind. I felt balanced, strong, stable, secure and safe, able to handle my daily struggles and adversities with evenness and resilience. This was because I had been reconnected to life, literally reattached to the roots of life, through him. This was the only cure for the disconnection in my life, which had appropriately manifested itself on the physical level as a "connective" tissue disease. Robert was part of this karmic rebalancing and I saw him and honored him as such: a very special person, an angel, an emissary from spirit.

My dream was for us to be together full-time as loving and healing partners. We discussed the possibility of living together in light of the strict environmental requirements and restrictions we each had to follow, and our individual housing situations and locations. But it wasn't to be. Gradually his health began to fail. His visits became erratic, and we saw less and less of each other. My heart broke as I realized I was losing him. And in the spring of 2009 I did. He passed away. I was devastated. Just like that, I lost everything that had become my world. The pattern had repeated itself.

Now I'm alone and isolated once again. But I am happy and grateful that for even just a little while, I got to experience love with a remarkable man. It was, and remains, the most important relationship of my life, and I will treasure it in my heart forever.

22

Progression of Silicone Poisoning

Despite my isolation and loneliness, being settled in my own safe house was a lifesaver. I no longer had to worry about chemical and electrical dangers because I had total control of my environment. This, however, did not mean my medical odyssey was over. As an experimental subject of the silicone gel and breast implant manufacturers, I am a living human example of how silicone poisoning progresses in the human body over time. And, unfortunately, silicone has indeed continued to affect me in new and unsuspected ways.

In 2008 my back problems took a turn for the worse. I was on one of my sporadic 20-minute walks through my neighborhood, when all of a sudden, it felt like the left side of my back collapsed. I dragged myself home and went to bed. It took several days of rest to recover. When I went to my doctor, he referred me to a specialist who diagnosed me as having degenerative disk disease, a condition in which the spongy disks between the spinal vertebrae dry out and flatten, causing pain and dysfunction. Intervertebral disks are composed of cartilage, which happens to be a connective tissue, a favorite target of silicone. In my case, more than likely the cartilage was adversely affected by the silicone, adding one more disease to my list of ailments.

While I was in Dallas I learned I had osteopenia, which is the precursor to osteoporosis. At the time I was only 43 years old and this information perplexed me. Wasn't I too young for this condition? I was not aware then that breast implants were to blame. I was so overwhelmed just trying to survive and deal with chemical and electrical reactions that I hadn't kept up with information about silicone. Consequently, I didn't know about <u>Torn Illusions</u>, a book by Pamela Stott-Kendall, which documents all the medical and scientific research, studies and data available on silicone and breast implants (see Appendix B).

By 2007 I had full-blown osteoporosis and by 2009 it had become severe, extremely unusual for someone my age. My local doctors, uninformed about silicone, speculated on the possible causes and prescribed first calcium and vitamin D, and then medication, none of which I tolerated. When I read <u>Torn Illusions</u> I discovered there are substances called cyclics in silicone gel that are by-products of the chemical manufacturing process. These can obstruct or derail calcium metabolism leading to accelerated osteoporosis. Now due to this excessive depletion of bone mass I am at very high risk for fractures, and have already suffered fragility fractures in the ribs several times, but have no choice except to live with this new and untreatable condition.

Silicone is an extremely toxic and dangerous substance which impacts every person who is exposed to it, whether in a silicone gel-filled prosthesis, a saline-filled prosthesis, or any number of solid state devices such as jaw or testicular implants. The latency period for some silicone-associated diseases can be very long, explaining why some individuals don't have any perceived health problems until many, many years later. Even then they may never link them to silicone.

Human hyperreactivity to silicone is another issue. It is possible some people's systems mount a greater and faster response to it, resulting in more aggressive and destructive disease.

The quality of the devices is yet another factor which determines the course of disease. In silicone gel breast implants there are two components: the silicone gel and the silicone elastomer shell. According to <u>Torn Illusions</u>, numerous irregularities were discovered in the manufacturing process of each of these, as evidenced in the flaws and discrepancies found between implants which were explanted from women and examined by toxicologists. Most crucial is the oven temperature for turning liquid silicone into gel. Deviations from the correct temperature resulted in dangerous changes in chemistry, which rendered more virulence to certain batches of gel, explaining the more severe and even lethal reactions in some patients.

There is no way for me to prove it, but I feel I may have received a set of implants from a more adulterated manufacturing series, which sent my body into violent reactions, especially after the shell ruptured in December 1988. This is evident to me particularly in the incessant advance of my chemical sensitivities. Most people with MCS do not present with such an advancing symptomatology. Their symptoms either stabilize at a particular level or fluctuate according to exposures. My MCS became so extreme it forced me 2500 miles away from family and into an existence of seclusion. Upon reaching its limit, it diverged into electrical sensitivity.

When I got to Prescott I was finally released from the electrical agony that had afflicted me at the Seagoville camp. I realized I continued to be electrically sensitive, but being in a more stable environment gave me the confidence that perhaps now my EHS would not progress.

My house came equipped with a gas furnace that I didn't tolerate and couldn't use. I spent a lot of time researching various heating systems with which to replace it. Each had to be eliminated for one reason or another, until I was left with the only option—an electric heating/air conditioning roof unit. Other E.I.'s had this type of furnace, and I thought I would do well with it. I couldn't have been more wrong.

It was a disaster. After a tremendous expenditure of money, time and precious energy, I was devastated by the reactions I suffered from the unit. They included nervous vibration and buzzing of my entire body, irritability and anger, worsened insomnia, violent dreams, depression and reactivation of systemic viruses. I shut down the unit, disconnected the power to it, and turned off the breakers in the electrical box. I've never used it again. In the winter months I close off my bedroom, kitchen and bath, and use small low-wattage space heaters. This system does not provide nearly enough heat, so I regularly wear my winter coat and hat indoors. This is the way I'm forced to live as a result of advanced electrical sensitivity due to silicone poisoning.

In 2008 in anticipation of the federally mandated switch to digital TV transmission, I bought a flat digital TV to replace the old 13-inch black and white TV I had been using. I had purchased the black and white TV second-hand from a woman who had severe allergies and whose house was spotless and devoid of chemicals and fragrances, thus it had not absorbed any odors and was safe for me. But because of its age and obsolete technology, it could not be converted to the new system.

In spite of running and outgassing the new TV outdoors for several months, it continued to be too toxic for me. The plastics, chemicals and components in newer TVs are much more noxious than the ones used in older models. I would need to encase the TV in a special TV box, just like the ones at the camp in Seagoville. So I had one made and installed outside my bedroom window. It was exciting to finally have color TV again, and as a bonus I ordered cable service, something I had not enjoyed since my New Jersey days. Both would help alleviate my isolation and boredom.

Of course I should have known it was too good to be true. After a few days of watching my new TV, I started feeling very destabilized and irritable. In the ensuing days I experienced headaches, visual disturbances, hyperacusis (abnormal hearing), wild dreams, and what I can only describe as a scrambled brain. I also felt wired, hyper and aggressive. EHS had struck again. I disconnected everything and waited for my symptoms to subside. Eventually I determined that my hyperreactions pertain to both cable and the color aspect of TV. And the digital technology, being the same as in computers, is definitely off limits to me.

Once again I felt devastated. Would the losses ever end? The digital deadline was extended from February to June 2009. This gave me a reprieve of four months. But I dreaded the arrival of June and the end of my TV watching days, which meant even more disconnection from the world. It felt like a death. When June arrived and my black and white analog TV continued to operate as before, I was flummoxed. I called the TV stations and was told that rural areas like Prescott, which get their TV reception through translators, don't have the same deadline compliance requirement as metropolitan areas. I had been granted another reprieve, possibly of several years. What a relief!

As I write this, it is November 2011 and I've had almost two and a half extra years of TV watching, but just this past weekend I lost four channels and am now down to three. Soon all television access will vanish from my life forever. This is one more repercussion of progressive electrical sensitivity due to silicone poisoning.

Compared to the rest of the world, I live in the Stone Age. There is no social media for me, no internet research, no e-mail, no texting, no e-books, no cell phones, no DVDs. I don't even get to view family photos. I am an outcast many times over.

The disadvantages to being trapped in a small southwestern town are too numerous to count, but the biggest one for me is probably the lack of silicone experts and environmental doctors. Each time a new problem crops up that I know is related to my silicone poisoning, I have no way to verify it or get the appropriate diagnosis. Without the proper medical professionals to coordinate my care, I always have to be my own detective/diagnostician. This is tough to do, especially without internet access, and I end up relying solely on my intuition. This is exactly what happened starting in August 2009.

I woke up one morning completely brain-fogged and unable to get out of bed. When I finally managed to get up, I wasn't able to think clearly or decide what to do next. I felt confused, and this alarmed me. In all my years of disability, I had never before lost the executive functions of my brain. In addition, I soon developed a fierce headache, hot flashes and sweating. These symptoms continued day after day and I surmised they might be hormone related, so I went to my gynecologist who tested my levels. Sure enough my estrogen levels had plummeted.

Through the years I had dealt with ongoing hormonal irregularities and upheavals, sometimes producing brain symptoms. They first showed up as a deficiency in testosterone, then in progesterone, and later in DHEA. It seemed that each time I worked to remedy a deficiency, a new one would ensue. What I didn't know for a long time is that silicone attracts and absorbs hormones and creates imbalances and disregulation of the hormonal system. Now I was desperate to restore my brain functions, and having had some success with hormone replacement in the past, I felt that estrogen would surely help. Instead I experienced bad reactions to it. My gynecologist didn't know what to do for me, and I was too impaired to figure out what to do next. Over the course of many months I literally stumbled here and there, grasping at straws, consulting various local practitioners who didn't have a clue, while struggling terribly with reduced brain function. It was one of my worst crises.

Concurrent with this new set of brain symptoms, I was having eye problems: dry eyes, blurry vision and double vision. My ophthalmologist wasn't concerned—he sees these problems all the time. But I was. I suspected these were neurological symptoms, and I finally put two and two together and realized that, in addition to hormonal deficiencies, I was dealing with a new neurological condition in my brain.

Now all I had to do was find a doctor who would agree to send me for an MRI, a magnetic resonance imaging, instead of deeming it an unnecessary medical expenditure based on his incomplete understanding of my illness, which was a situation I had faced before. I tried my local rheumatologist and it worked: I was able to convince him to order the expensive test. The results were sobering: white matter lesions in the frontal lobes. Of all my diagnoses, this one scares me the most. It portends the continued loss of the brain's ability to plan, think, organize, initiate and make decisions. It was this diagnosis which spurred me to write this memoir. Fearing I don't have much time left, I want to leave my story behind to inform and benefit others.

When I went to the library in 1977 looking for books on breast implants to help me decide on their safety, this is the kind of book I wish I had found.

23

Final Thoughts and Reflections

After receiving my brain lesions diagnosis, I was relieved to finally have an answer, and set out to find a solution. Eventually I was fortunate to find a pure form of the antioxidant CoQ10, short for coenzyme Q10, which increased the blood circulation to my brain and restored some of its executive functions. The cobwebs were dispelled, and the sensation of having cotton balls in my forehead in the place of brain matter was gone. My nerve synapses started firing again, not exactly like before, but enough to help me think clearly once again.

Still, the idea of writing a book, which had always seemed too forbidding and overwhelming to me, was not something I felt capable of doing, or was even considering. What I knew I should do is use and exercise my brain to try to prevent further deterioration or at least delay it. This was a huge dilemma, in that it is virtually impossible to do so without the benefit of some kind of stimulation from other people, the internet, or the outside world. The only outlet I had left was library books, which a library volunteer would drop off periodically and leave under my carport. Books have been my only steady companions but like everything else, without being able to share and discuss them with others, their value to the health of the brain, and indeed to one's overall life is limited.

Ultimately what inspired me to write was <u>The Autobiography of Benjamin Franklin</u>. He became my hero when I learned he started the first public library in Philadelphia. Without him there might not be a public library system in the U.S., which in my estimation is a national treasure. Unable to do my own research, I have utilized the capable assistance of the reference librarians at my local library countless times. During the course of writing my memoir, I have called them dozens, if not hundreds, of times.

Benjamin Franklin wrote the first half of his autobiography in only nine days. It struck me that if a luminary such as he, with an accomplished, prodigious and distinguished career, could write about his life in such an expeditious and brief manner, maybe I could do something similar. There was no need to think writing a book had to be a daunting proposition, or take years to execute. One morning in December 2010 I got up, sat at my desk and started writing: I would tell my story simply and openly, in my own words, at my own pace. I would need more than nine days though, so I gave myself one year. In order not to overload my circuits and feel swamped, I decided to set a modest goal of writing an average of one paragraph per day.

This was a manageable project. It gave me a way to exercise my brain without overtaxing it. It also gave me a daily purpose, and a means to express myself in a new way. Indeed it was the last method available to me to communicate with and reach out to the outside world. Writing long-hand had always been something I enjoyed and preferred over typing anyway, so that was not a problem. The problem would be finding a fragrance-free typist who would not contaminate my manuscript.

Initially my title was going to be <u>A Chemical Injury Memoir</u> because I wanted people to understand that I was struck by chemical injury, and it just happened to be via silicone poisoning. Others have been hit by chemical injury through Gulf War Syndrome. Still others were felled during the clean-up of Ground Zero after 9/11, and the clean-up of the Exxon Valdez oil spill, and that of the BP oil spill in the Gulf of Mexico. Chemical injury happens in airtight, energy efficient "sick" buildings, and in formaldehyde-laden FEMA trailers provided for the victims of Hurricane Katrina. It strikes through exposure to aerial pesticide spraying, and daily use of synthetic perfumes and fragranced products. Every day people are chemically injured all around the world in a multitude of ways from all kinds of chemicals.

But this isn't something we talk about or concede for what it is: a world overly exposed to and overly reliant on chemicals. If we are willing to accept such a level of chemical infiltration in our lives, we should also be willing to talk realistically about its consequences and dangers. We must be informed and we must demand full disclosure. And most of all we must acknowledge and understand the suffering of the victims because, after all, we are the sacrificial lambs, the collateral damage for the conveniences and lifestyles everyone else enjoys. We should be honored and thanked for our "service", not shunned and forgotten.

In our society we celebrate those who recover from their wounds and heal from their diseases, and rejoin society. We give them our attention and accolades. But what about those of us who are crippled for life by chemicals? What about those of us who can't rejoin society; who are segregated, isolated and disenfranchised to extreme extents due to chemical injury? We are the real heroes, struggling daily on our own, fighting everything and everyone alone, courageous warriors in a world of toxic dangers, indifference and greed, a world that still would like to deny our illnesses and the care we deserve. The message seems to be: if you get injured and can't recover, you are on your own. This is wrong. It's time to incorporate a discourse on chemical injury into our daily lives and into our national dialogue.

Why don't we ask ourselves, for example, why there is such an epidemic of autism among our children, and of attention deficit disorder and attention deficit hyperactivity disorder among our teenagers? Why are Alzheimer's and Parkinson's disease so prevalent among our senior citizens? Why do chronic fatigue syndrome and fibromyalgia strike so many people in the prime of their lives? My sense is that all of these conditions, as well as many others, have a relationship with some sort of chemical injury. Subtle or overt, obvious or not, chemical injury permeates all of our lives and affects everyone. It is time to wake up and take notice.

When I first looked for books on silicone breast implants, there weren't very many. The few I discovered had the words "silicone" or "breast implants" in their titles. Yet one of the most informative ones, <u>Torn Illusions</u> by Pamela Stott-Kendall, did not, and only appeared after I did much digging and made lots of phone calls. Although my memoir is a tribute to all severely chemically injured individuals all over the world, I realized that if I wanted women to easily find my book, it would have to have a more precise title, so I called it <u>Silicone Injury</u>. To honor the courage and the journey of other silicone-injured women, I have gathered together all the books written by them and about them that I was able to find, and have included them in Appendix B.

A few weeks ago I was listening to National Public Radio where the conversation centered around "dignity therapy," a new approach being used to help those at the end of life. The participants in this therapy write or dictate their life story to leave behind a record of their influence on the world. This helps them to feel that they mattered and will continue to matter, and not that they are simply disappearing from the planet. I realized that this is exactly what I am doing with my memoir.

The only difference is that I have already disappeared from the planet. I am completely unseen and unheard. This is my attempt to sort of raise myself from the dead, and be noticed and acknowledged for my experience. Have I had an influence on the world? I don't feel that I have because I feel so invisible and irrelevant. But writing my story has been cathartic and strengthening, and has helped to remind me that we all impact the world in a myriad of ways, known and unknown.

I don't know if my story will elicit the understanding and compassion I wish from the people in my life and the rest of the world. The fact is I am still looking for my community, my tribe, a world to belong to, because as things stand I am a world of one. Maybe only the future readers of my story will be that tribe, fellow sufferers from across time and space. Maybe only they can relate and empathize. If so, then the purpose of this memoir will have been fulfilled and that will be my small imprint on the planet.

APPENDIX A

Update on Silicone Breast Implants

Since the 1992 FDA moratorium on silicone gel breast implants, the popularity of breast augmentation with saline implants has skyrocketed. Women have been lulled into thinking that saline-filled breast implants are safe. But not only do they pose the same dangers as gel-filled implants, they also produce very specific systemic infections characteristic only of saline implants. These are discussed in Dr. Susan E. Kolb's book, <u>The Naked Truth about Breast Implants</u> (see Appendix B).

In 2006, 14 years after the FDA ban, the only two remaining breast implant manufacturers applied to the FDA for approval to bring gel implants back on the market. The manufacturers still had not conducted long-term studies, established a patient registry, or complied with other FDA directives. Unbelievably, despite objections and recommendations to the contrary from many experts, the FDA granted their request. The approvals were conditional on new requirements for post-approval studies, tracking and evaluations.

In June 2011 the FDA issued an updated report on the status of breast implants, which can be found at its website (see Appendix B). While still reassuring the public that breast implants have a "reasonable assurance of safety," the FDA now admits that they are associated with significant local complications and adverse outcomes, with a large percentage of them, up to 70%, failing and requiring reoperation and removal in 8-10 years. They further state that the longer a woman has breast implants, the more likely she is to experience problems, and will need to monitor them for the rest of her life. The recommendation is for MRI screening three years after implantation, and every two years thereafter to check for ruptures. In addition, the minimum age required to receive implants is now 22. I received mine at the age of 20: I wonder how my destiny would have changed if I'd had to wait another two years.

A warning was issued that women with both gel and saline implants have a small but increased likelihood of developing a rare form of cancer of the immune system, anaplastic large cell lymphoma. Yet when it comes to autoimmune and rheumatic diseases, immunological and neurological conditions, and other systemic illnesses, the FDA continues to claim there is no apparent association between them and breast implants, even while acknowledging that the manufacturers' post-approval studies do not provide adequate data to make such an evaluation. They also acknowledge that the post-approval studies are of very short duration and have had very low follow-up rates, meaning that problems have undoubtedly been underreported.

In The Naked Truth about Breast Implants, Dr. Susan Kolb relates how women who participated in the studies were told by those conducting the studies that their systemic symptoms had nothing to do with their implants. Other women were apparently released from the studies when they became ill. It looks like it is business as usual at the implant manufacturers' and plastic surgeons' offices.

Nevertheless, I feel that we are getting somewhere. If women read the complete FDA report, it will give them food for thought, and much more information than I had available 35 years ago. Hopefully it will allow them to make a more informed, intelligent decision, not one based on wishful thinking or the obfuscations still prevalent in the marketing and promotional materials for breast implants. However, women need to get all the facts, and the history of silicone provides those facts.

Silicone was first used in humans in the 1940's by Japanese doctors who injected the liquid form to augment the breasts of prostitutes. Later American doctors did the same for Las Vegas show girls. The results were catastrophic. As reported in the Institute of Medicine's <u>Information for Women about the Safety of Silicone Breast Implants</u>, published in 2000 (see Appendix B), the complications were relentlessly progressive. They led to severe injuries like acute pneumonitis, pulmonary embolisms, ulcerations, infections, necrosis, gangrene, disfigurement, liver dysfunction, cancers, coma and death. Due to these dangers, silicone injections became illegal in Japan in the late 1940's.

By the 1950's American manufacturers developed silicone for all kinds of industrial applications. They should have stopped there. Instead they went on to produce medical devices, such as joint replacements. Problems became apparent right away and the first animal studies were conducted which proved that silicone produces immunological, inflammatory and toxic reactions. Yet they kept this information to themselves, and in the 1960's developed the first breast implant by enclosing a gel form of silicone inside a silastic silicone shell. In the 1970's, when silicone injections finally became illegal in the U.S., breast implants were modified to be softer with a more fluid gel and a thinner shell.

Liquid silicone had been classified as a drug and been under the control of the FDA. Breast implants on the other hand, even though composed of the same exact substance, were classified as medical devices and were not under the regulation or scrutiny of any regulatory agency at that time. They slipped through and were marketed as safe. Left unchecked, they went on to enjoy increasing popularity into the 1980's, until all the injuries and illnesses surfaced, reaching critical mass in 1992.

Now 20 years have passed. This would have been enough time for a long-term study which would have definitively resolved the issue of the association between silicone breast implants and systemic disease, if only one had been formulated and carried out. Instead the time was squandered. The reality is that the evidence already exists in the form of clinical, toxicological and research data, to show the linkage between implants and serious disease, but it doesn't seem to convince or satisfy the FDA. This only means one thing: more time will pass with even more women being needlessly sacrificed.

APPENDIX B

References, Books, and Resources

I. Silicone Breast Implants

Stott-Kendall, Pamela. <u>Torn Illusions – Fully Documented Private and Public Expose' of the Worldwide Medical Tragedy of Silicone Implants</u>. Fort Lauderdale, FL: Debcar Publishing, 1996. This well researched book is out of print but can still be found on Amazon. com. The 1994 edition subtitled "One Woman's Tragic Experience with the Silicone Conspiracy" can be found in the public library system.

Kolb, Susan E., M.D. <u>The Naked Truth About Breast Implants – From Harm to Healing.</u> Savage, MN: Lone Oak Publishing, 2010. <u>www.plastikos. com</u> (770)457-4677. The author is both a plastic surgeon and an implant patient. As a "wounded healer", her medical practice treats thousands of silicone-injured women.

United States. Food and Drug Administration. "FDA Update on the Safety of Silicone

Gel-Filled Breast Implants". June 2011. www.fda.gov/cdrh/breastimplants

United States. Institute of Medicine. Information for Women about the Safety of Silicone Breast Implants. Ed. Martha Grigg, Stuart Bondurant, Virginia L. Ernster, Roger Herdman. Washington, D.C.: National Academies Press, 2000.

National Research Center for Women and Families, 1001 Connecticut Avenue NW, Suite 1100, Washington DC 20036. (202)223-4000 www.breastimplantinfo.org/about.html

Leighland, Diana. Big Breasts to Die for – The Silicone Survivors Handbook. 2005 www.siliconesurvivors.com 1-800-795-3069. In this e-book the author recounts how she healed from silicone injury with natural methods.

Helman, Susan A. Pope. Toxic Silicone Poisoning – The True Breast Implant Stories. Bloomington, IN: Authorhouse, 2004. This book includes many women's personal stories, detailed information about the chemicals used in breast implants, the public relations campaign used by manufacturers, and more.

Stewart, Mary White. Silicone Spills – Breast Implants on Trial. Westport, CT: Praeger Publisher, 1998. The author is a sociologist who served as jury consultant for an injured woman in a high-profile case. She discusses legal and sociological issues, and presents many women's personal stories.

Bywalec, Gloria L. and Rzeppa, Anna Marie. <u>Betrayed</u>. Canton, MI: JMJ Publishing, 1996. A short personal story incorporating poetry.

Wonder, Vanity. <u>Shot Girls.</u> Bloomington, IN: Authorhouse, 2012. A fascinating, first-person account of the world of illegal, black-market silicone injections used by strippers and dancers to enlarge their buttocks.

II. Multiple Chemical Sensitivity/Environmental Illness (MCS/EI) and Electromagnetic Hypersensitivity (EHS)

Evans, Jerry. <u>Chemical and Electrical Hypersensitivity – A Sufferer's Memoir</u>. Jefferson, NC: McFarland, 2010.

Gibson, Pamela Reed, Ph.D. <u>Multiple Chemical Sensitivity – A Survival Guide</u>. Oakland, CA: New Harbinger Publications, 2000.

Mann, Arnold. <u>They're Poisoning Us! From the Gulf War to the Gulf of Mexico – An Investigative Report</u>. Los Angeles, CA: 34th Street Press, 2011.

Alison Johnson has written several books and produced several videos on MCS. <u>www.</u>

alisonjohnsonmcs.com www.chemicalsensitivity
foundation.org

Chemical Injury Information Network, P.O.
Box 301, White Sulphur Springs MT 59645,
USA. (406)547-2255 www.ciin.org. A nonprofit
membership organization with a monthly
publication called "Our Toxic Times".

III. Chronic Fatigue Syndrome (CFS)

Munson, Peggy ed. Stricken – Voices from the
Hidden Epidemic of CFS. New York, NY:
Hawthorn Press, 2000.

The CFIDS Association of America, P.O.
Box 220398, Charlotte NC 28222-0398.
(704)365-2343 www.cfids.org

IV. Fibromyalgia (FM)

Fibromyalgia Network, P.O. Box 31750, Tucson
AZ 85751-1750. 1-800-853-2929 www.
fmnetnews.com